ENTERTAINING
WITH CHARM

A MODERN GUIDE TO
RELAXED GATHERINGS

EDEN PASSANTE

PHOTOGRAPHY BY ZAN PASSANTE

weldon**owen**

TO ROMEO AND MONROE

You two are what dreams are made of! You love a sweet treat as much as your mama, and you have been my little recipe testers since you could eat solids. I love you both with all my heart and am so thankful I get to be your mama. You have inspired me in a million ways, and I hope this book inspires you both to become little entertainers!

CONTENTS

INTRODUCTION

Welcome to your guide to having friends and family over and keeping it fun, simple, and, of course, charming! This book is filled with year-round recipes that are both easy to make and great for company. Whether hosting a casual but cozy gathering or a big holiday celebration, this guide covers tips on adding charm to your get-togethers.

We all know that hosting can be stressful, but it doesn't have to be. My goal is to inspire you to have company over, even if you order in. Inviting friends for social gatherings can increase your happiness and overall well-being. This book teaches you how to keep things simple while making your guests feel amazing in a welcoming and cozy environment. There is an art to it; luckily, it's pretty simple. I am also sharing some of my favorite recipes for appetizers, mains, sides, desserts, snacks, and drinks, all of which are guaranteed to please your guests.

But here's the best part: this book isn't about following strict rules. Forget the old way of entertaining—of focusing on perfection and complicated dishes. My approach is about relaxing with your friends and family and having good conversations, all while sipping a darn delicious cocktail! You don't need to cook a four-course meal to host a casual get-together, birthday, or even an impressive holiday party. Some of my best times are shared at home with a few friends late into the evening, and guess what? The food and beverage are often simply a large cheese and charcuterie board and a nice wine. It's all about getting together, setting a beautiful scene, having a good time, and doing it with added charm to make your guests feel extra special.

ABOUT ME AND
SUGAR AND CHARM

This isn't one of those books by an author who grew up cooking alongside a mother or grandmother in the kitchen. Nor is it a collection of treasured family recipes passed down through generations. Neither situation matches my reality. Although my passion for easy, good food and charming entertaining *did* spark from my childhood, it was more of an escape.

I gleefully turned to the arts, baking, and crafting as a retreat from an often rocky childhood. I know that I'll be forever grateful for the free community art and craft classes I came across, which were a catalyst for this unique field. Now, many years later, it's a very magical (and sometimes shocking) feeling to be publishing my first book.

The kitchen has been where I can let everything go and focus solely on whatever I'm making. After years of using the kitchen as a blank canvas, I've also learned that working in it is a form of meditation and of being in the present. This means focusing on the perfect scoop of flour, watching the paddle whip soft butter until creamy, and physically creating something delicious I can dive into once it's done. I've always loved that I can start with simple ingredients and make a beautiful and (usually) edible creation that didn't exist before I started. It has been something I can control and take pride in, especially that first bite of fluffy cake with creamy frosting.

Growing up, I would get lost in baking supply stores, picking out new sprinkles, dyes, and fondant. I still do, but now I also hit up the local cheese shop and a well-curated liquor store. I've always had a sweet tooth, but more importantly, I love what baked goods and delicious candies have represented in my life: celebration, creativity, fun, and nostalgia.

I was always creative. I'd sit in my bedroom for hours sculpting clay figures (I sculpted a clay figure of my pregnant fifth-grade teacher and gave it to her!), mini food items, and animals. I took every art and craft class available in my tiny coastal hometown: pastels, watercolor, sewing, ceramics—you name it, I was into it! I did not excel in traditional school, eventually graduating from an alternative high school and then moving to Los Angeles two weeks after my eighteenth birthday.

After initially tossing the idea of college out the window, I found a program at California State University, Northridge, called family and consumer science, which is modern-day home economics. It was an aha moment for me. Maybe I could give more schooling a chance? I studied food science, cooking, nutrition, sewing, art, child development, and family studies. I *loved* the major, and at the time, I had no idea it would be so pivotal in my future career.

Right around college graduation, I got engaged, began planning my wedding, and stumbled upon something I knew nothing about: wedding blogs, design blogs, and mommy blogs—oh my! I suddenly found myself immersed in a fascinating new industry that had just begun. It was a creative outlet where regular people like me were sharing ideas on art and design, weddings, flowers, and more. I read a collection of blogs for hours every day and eventually started my own blog, *Sugar and Charm*, in 2010.

The evolution has been entirely organic. What began as a wedding blog for me became a lifestyle, DIY, and baking blog, which eventually turned into an entertaining-focused recipe site. There was never a business plan. I, along with all the other early home-focused bloggers, were figuring it out as we went. I adored my newfound hobby and creative outlet as I embarked on a new chapter: marriage.

I dreamt of a stable family, being a mom, a special home, and a career that allowed me to be creative. I marveled at the thought of parties at my house, gatherings with friends and family, baking delicious homemade cakes for my kids, and creating magical holidays in a cozy but magazine-worthy home. I knew I would have to work hard for this, and I was willing to put in the effort to make my dreams come true.

So here I am several years, three hundred parties, one thousand photo shoots, five hundred cakes, three houses, fifteen years married, two handsome children, a cherished career, and one book later. Life is a lovely and challenging roller coaster. Fortunately, I've had some incredible role models who have shown

me what success looks like and rooted for me since the beginning. Words can't express my respect and admiration for those people.

I feel beyond grateful that I get to share my creative ideas and recipes with so many of you. Honestly, I couldn't have wished for a better career than this one, which has allowed me to connect with people all over the world through my work. Luckily, my passion for hosting gatherings, sipping a whimsical cocktail, and baking a homemade dessert can never be satiated. It's where I find joy in this crazy, wonderful life, and the way food, drinks, and easy entertaining bring people together is what it's all about—life's simple pleasures. I love it.

WHAT ENTERTAINING
MEANS TO ME

Charming Atmosphere. Candles, low lights, fresh flowers, linen napkins, and a welcome cocktail should be part of nearly every gathering. These are simple to arrange and make a massive difference to any get-together, big or small. Setting a pretty scene is straightforward. It's easy to pick (or purchase) fresh flowers, light candles, and invest in a beautiful linen tablecloth and napkins. It's about using natural elements—what's in my garden?—to add charm in a way anyone can do.

Resources. It's about tapping into your resources and using them. Small space or budget? No problem. Use what you have to entertain anywhere: the park, the beach, or a community courtyard.

Imperfections. It's okay for things to go wrong. In fact, I like to allow for imperfections at a party as they add character, charm, and personality to your gathering. It's not about making every element of an event perfect or elaborate. I've had many things go wrong when I'm hosting. One time, I forgot to put sugar in a friend's birthday cake, which made for a lot of laughs and a funny story years later. Hosting a party should be fun, and trying to achieve perfection will create stress. So instead I embrace the little mishaps and imperfections that happen at every gathering. Overcooked meatballs? No biggie—just add extra sauce. The

chicken dish needs more time to cook? Put out more snacks and serve dinner later. Bad weather? Bring it indoors and create a cozy ambiance. As long as you laugh it off and keep your spirits high, your guests will too.

Feeling. If I could scream this to the world, I would. The most essential part of being around others, especially in your home, is making them feel welcome. Maya Angelou said it best: "I've learned that people will forget what you said, people will forget what you did, but people will never forget how you made them feel." This is true in all aspects of life, especially when you invite friends into your home.

Sense of Pride. I have a sense of pride, ownership, and satisfaction when I create an inviting space to bring people together over food and drink, and watching them enjoy themselves always makes my heart burst!

High-Low. I love to mix things up. The same high-low aesthetic that is popular in fashion—Target jeans with Jimmy Choo flats—can also apply to entertaining. You can order fried chicken from the best spot in town and then serve one of your favorite high-end Champagnes. (If you didn't already know, let me assure you fried chicken and Champagne are beautiful together.) Something I do often is order from a local restaurant but make a fabulous cocktail, simple appetizer, and dessert.

Keeping It Simple. Your guests, family, and friends won't have more fun if you have spent days in the kitchen stressing over complicated recipes. They will have just as much fun with a thoughtfully planned, easy-to-assemble menu, festive drinks, and a charming atmosphere with the attention on them. *This is the recipe for a successful gathering.* Remember the candles, flowers, and a few attentive touches, such as water readily available for your guests to grab. If you're hosting an outdoor gathering, have bug repellant, blankets, or anything else that would make guests more comfortable visibly arranged in the setting. This way, they can get what they need without having to ask.

EDEN'S ESSENTIALS

Here are the things I regularly use when entertaining. They are divided into three categories: kitchen, which covers pots, pans, and cooking tools; hosting, which includes everything from candles and three-tier serving trays to glassware and table linens; and pantry, which lists the ingredients that I always have on hand for entertaining.

KITCHEN ESSENTIALS

- Cast-iron pan
- Large and small skillets
- Large, medium, and small saucepans
- Two 9-inch and 8-inch round cake pans
- 10-inch Bundt pan
- 13 x 18-inch sheet pan
- 1 or 2 cookie sheets
- Stand mixer
- Handheld mixer
- Food processor
- Blender, preferably high-powered
- Slow cooker
- Mixing bowls
- Salad spinner
- Cutting boards
- Chef's knife
- Paring knife
- Wooden spoons and spatulas
- Slotted spoon
- Rubber and silicone spatulas
- Whisk
- Citrus zester
- Citrus juicer
- Garlic press
- Large and small fine-mesh strainers
- Measuring cups and spoons
- Instant-read thermometer

PANTRY ESSENTIALS

- Miso paste
- Chile crunch oil
- Butterfly pea flowers
- Truffle oil
- Smoky salt
- Flaky sea salt
- Panko (Japanese bread crumbs)
- Sesame seeds
- Ground cardamom
- Colorful sprinkles
- Calabrian chiles
- Castelvetrano olives (serve these on their own or add to a cheese/charcuterie platter)
- Canned cannellini beans
- Rao's Homemade Marinara Pasta Sauce
- Olive oil and coconut oil
- Apple cider vinegar
- Hot honey
- Instant espresso powder
- Pure vanilla extract
- Pure almond extract

- Linen napkins and tablecloth or table runner
- Cocktail napkins: I often buy pretty paper cocktail napkins when I see them as they always come in handy; I like linen cocktail napkins as well.
- Fancy flatware: I keep a full set of forks and knives stored away for parties. They're gold and not great for everyday use, so I use them, hand wash and dry them, and save them for the next gathering.
- Large serving platters and bowls
- Small plates or boards
- Marble cheese platter
- Wooden serving boards
- Mason jars (for flowers, drinks, desserts, and even votives)

- Three-tier serving tray
- Votive candles (many!)
- Taper candles and holders (lots and lots!)
- Cocktail glasses: Have a set of at least twelve to use for smaller gatherings.
- Wineglasses: You'll want good-quality ones. Never use those super-thick ones, please.
- Plant-based disposable cups: These are great for larger gatherings when I don't want to wash a million dishes.
- Disposable bamboo plates: These are study and look classier than paper plates. I use them all the time.
- Bamboo knot picks: Eco-friendly and easy to grasp, these picks are perfect for garnishing drinks and for picking up hors d'oeuvres.

EDEN'S GUIDE TO ENTERTAINING

As I have already mentioned, there are no rules when it comes to entertaining. However, there is an art to being a good host and having a smooth gathering. Here are some ways to ensure success whenever you bring people together.

TIPS FOR A PROBLEM-FREE GATHERING

1. I try to finish everything that needs to be done for the get-together before my guests arrive. That way, I can relax and focus on greeting them. If I am still arranging the table or trying to finish a recipe as people are coming in, I cannot do what is essential, which is make my guests feel welcome.

2. Always have a cocktail (or mocktail) ready for guests as they walk in. Whether you've prepared a festive punch or set up a cocktail bar, it's important to have an area where guests can get a drink right away.

3. Keep the menu simple. The more elaborate your choices are, the more anxious you will be when preparing them, and the less fun the party will be.

4. Wait to serve dessert. Let your guests digest and relax a bit before piling on another course.

5. Never start to clean up while your guests are still present. Trust me, I know it's all fun and games until someone (me or my husband) has to clean up. However, the mess is part of the joy of hosting. Wait until everyone leaves and then put on your favorite podcast and dive in. You can also hire someone, whether a high school student or someone through an agency, to do cleanup during the party. It is important that neither you nor your guests do any cleaning during the gathering.

6. People will remember how they feel in your home—the small details and the fun atmosphere. So go the extra mile to create a warm, inviting space—flowers, candles, a good playlist, low lighting—and keep that good feeling going until the last guest leaves.

AVOIDING STRESS

You will decide how stressful (or not) your gathering will be. And, yes, larger holiday parties and fancier dinners can be stressful, no matter the size. However, there are steps you can take to keep the stress level under control. I want to make entertaining fun for you so you will invite company over more often and relish in the joys of late-night chats, laughter, and memories made with your friends and family.

Here is the key to reducing stress whenever you entertain: anything you can do beforehand, do it. Don't save everything for the day of the party. Indeed, just writing that sentence stresses me out! Just as in life, preparation is vital. Here are my tips on how to prepare.

· Four to six weeks before the event, send out a text or an invite (via email) and mark your gathering on the calendar. If you're hosting a theme party, now is the time to pick the theme, such as a bonfire or a garden party. If you're just having company over, skip this part.

- A week before, ensure you have all your hosting essentials. If you need to order something, do it. Also, confirm who will attend.

- Three days before, put together the menu.

- Two days before, grocery shop for food and drinks. Remember, there are many delivery services, and you don't even have to step into a grocery store if you don't want to.

- One day before, prepare anything that can be made one day in advance. Almost everything can be prepped the day before (even two days before!), so do what you can to lighten the load on the day of the party.

- One day before, set the table, set out platters and other serveware, make the floral arrangements (or have them delivered), clean the house, and stock the restrooms.

- One day before, write down on sticky notes what goes in each platter and attach them to the dishes. This way, you'll know what goes in each one when you are ready to serve.

- Day of the party, wake up early and refreshed. You won't have much to do since you're so prepared! You can now start cooking and assembling. It is fine if you are ordering in. Just be sure to make it charming.

- Leave yourself 30 minutes before guests arrive to relax, pour a drink, and sit.

- Then enjoy your house party!

SHOPPING THE SEASONS

I designed this cookbook to be a year-round guide for gatherings. I developed recipes that are good to make every month on the calendar and work for all different kinds of occasions. You can find the ingredients in grocery stores and markets throughout the year.

However, I want to touch briefly on seasonality because using fresh produce and seasonal foods as much as possible is essential to hosting a charming gathering. It's also easy to do, as food shops and farmers' markets are filled with seasonal fruits and vegetables.

When you're shopping, always pick up fruits and vegetables at their peak of season. For example, purchase fresh figs, pomegranates, or persimmons for a cheese platter in the fall, or tomatoes, cucumbers, and crunchy bell peppers for a summer vegetable platter. When you make a savory main dish, serve it with a simple side of roasted seasonal vegetables, such as parsnips in fall, asparagus in spring, or zucchini in summer. These sides don't need to be complicated.

Spring: Apricots, cherries, strawberries, artichokes, asparagus, avocados, bell peppers, broccoli, carrots, fava beans, lettuce, peas, radishes, rhubarb

Summer: Blueberries, melons (honeydew, cantaloupe), nectarines, peaches, plums, raspberries, bell peppers, corn, cucumbers, eggplants, green beans, tomatoes, zucchini

Fall: Apples, grapes, pears, brussels sprouts, butternut squash, carrots, corn, eggplants, parsnips, pumpkins, sweet potatoes

Winter: Apples, citrus fruits (oranges, grapefruits, pomelos), pears, persimmons, avocados, beets, brussels sprouts, cabbage, carrots, kale, parsnips

HOW TO ADD CHARM TO FOOD

Would you believe me if I told you I keep a box filled with ways to add charm to my recipes and cocktails? It's stocked with natural, colorful powders, many sprinkles, dehydrated citrus fruits, and other fun things I pick up here and there.

It always makes me happy when I order a dish or a cocktail at a restaurant and it comes garnished with a beautiful edible flower or a dehydrated citrus slice. This light touch makes me smile, which is why I do the same thing for my guests.

Here are some simple ways you can add charm when entertaining.

CITRUS

Dehydrated citrus fruits are a simple and fun way to add charm to your recipes. I keep a stock of dehydrated orange, lemon, and lime slices on hand in airtight containers to use as a garnish for desserts, cocktails, and fruit and cheese platters. They also make great decorations. I like to string them and hang them around the house or add them to wreaths. Plus, they make great gifts. Here is the quick and easy method for dehydrating citrus fruits.

Preheat the oven to 200°F. Line a sheet pan with parchment paper. Slice the desired citrus fruits—lemons, limes, oranges, grapefruits, and so on—into ¼-inch-thick rounds. Arrange the slices in a single layer on the prepared pan. Bake the slices, checking and flipping them halfway through to ensure even drying time, for 4–5 hours. The slices are ready when they are fully dried and crisp. Let cool, then transfer to ziplock bags or other airtight containers and store at room temperature. They will keep for up to 3 months in an airtight container.

Citrus zest is one of the best ways to bring small touches of color, flavor, and charm to your favorite dishes and drinks. Using a grater or zester to add a little lemon, orange, lime, or grapefruit zest to a recipe imparts a bright, citrusy aroma that elevates the flavors of the foods without overpowering them.

EDIBLE FLOWERS

As you look through this book, you will see that I love using edible flowers in my dishes. They will contribute color, texture, and, of course, charm to almost anything you make. I regularly add them to cocktails, dips, desserts, and salads.

FRESH FLOWERS

Marigolds: These bright orange or yellow flowers have a subtle flavor and bring a good amount of color to a dish.

Nasturtiums: These bright, peppery, versatile flowers can be added to salads and sandwiches or used as a garnish on warm dishes.

Violets: Sweet and slightly lemony in flavor, violets make a great addition to spring salads, desserts, and syrups. They also make a lovely garnish for cakes and cupcakes.

Lavender: Fresh lavender imparts sweet floral notes to syrups, ice cream, and other desserts.

Pansies: Known for their pretty colors, these flowers are perfect for garnishing desserts and salads and for making floral ice cubes (page 23).

Borage: These star-shaped blue flowers have a mild cucumber flavor and are especially pretty scattered atop salads.

Roses: The petals of these iconic blooms can be used to give a sweet, floral flavor to everything from salads to rice to dessert syrups to butter for spreading on a favorite muffin.

Daisies: These dainty yet cheerful white-and-yellow flowers remind me of my childhood. I love adding them to desserts and cocktails.

Dandelions: The young, bright yellow, many-petaled blooms have a sweet flavor that especially complements salads and beverages.

Chrysanthemums: The mild, slightly spicy flavor of these showy blossoms makes them a welcome addition to salads.

DRIED FLOWERS

I keep dried flowers on hand too. You can order them online, and they last a long time when kept in a tightly capped jar or other airtight container. They're great to use in the winter when fresh flowers aren't readily available. Here are a few of my favorites:

- Rose petals
- Hibiscuses
- Pansies
- Lavender
- Lotus flowers
- Butterfly pea flowers
- Cornflower petals

FLORAL FINISHING SALT

MAKES ABOUT ½ CUP

½ cup flaky sea salt

3–4 tablespoons dried edible flowers of choice

In a small jar or tin, combine the salt and flowers, cap tightly, and shake gently to mix well. The salt will keep for several months in a cool place.

This is an easy way to add a little charm, flavor, and texture at the same time. Sprinkle this flower-flecked salt on appetizers, pasta, salads, cookies, and more. It also makes a beautiful going-home gift for your guests.

EDIBLE FLOWER GARDEN

Over the years, I've had multiple edible flower gardens. I've used outdoor pots and garden beds. And just as with an herb garden, I plant different flower varieties throughout the year. I grow according to the season, keeping in mind which flowers will tolerate the heat of summer or thrive in the cool days of fall, winter, and spring (it never gets too cold in Southern California). Here are the simple steps to set you on the path to an edible flower garden.

· Decide whether you want garden pots or a more extensive, dedicated garden bed.

· Fill the garden space with good-draining, nutrient-rich organic soil.

· Head to your local nursery with a list of edible flowers (for the season) and buy small plants that are already blooming. You don't need to start with seeds.

· Plant the flowers in the prepared soil, leaving enough room around each one for it to spread and grow.

· Water regularly by hand or use an automated drip system to maintain the water amounts.

· Prune your plants as needed and harvest the flowers when they are still fresh and lovely.

· Enjoy using your colorful blooms in dishes throughout the year.

HOW TO MAKE FLORAL ICE CUBES

Floral ice cubes will give your drinks an extra touch of color and fun. Plus, they are easy to make. You will need small fresh edible flowers, ice cube trays (I like to make large square cubes for cocktails), and filtered water.

Place a flower into each compartment of an ice-cube tray, pressing them lightly to secure them. (If the flowers are small, you can add more than one to each slot.) Fill the ice-cube tray with filtered water. Place the trays in the freezer until the water is frozen solid, at least 6 hours. When the ice cubes are ready, just pop them out and serve them in your favorite drinks.

Switch up your ice-cube centers with herbs and fruits for the holidays and the seasons. In winter, add rosemary and cranberries. In spring, I like to use small slices of citrus. Berries and other herbs, such as thyme and sage, are wonderful too.

NATURAL POWDERS

Natural powders, such as hibiscus, butterfly pea, and beet, are magical, as they allow you to add color and flavor to your dishes. Make sure any powders you buy are certified organic and free of artificial colors and additives. I like to mix these colorful powders into whipped cream or frosting or sprinkle them over desserts.

You can find natural powders in natural foods stores and online, and they keep well in an airtight container in a cool, dry, dark place for a few months or longer. If I were to buy four powders to always have in my box, it would be strawberry powder, açai powder, blue spirulina, and beet powder.

> EDEN'S TIP: *The ice cubes will turn pink if you use dried hibiscus flowers. You can boil water with butterfly pea flowers to make blue ice cubes.*

Easy Appetizers and Snacks

I am all about the snacks! Give me a giant cheese platter, some delicious dips, and a signature cocktail, and I'm ready for any party. Whether it's a game night with friends or a larger gathering, a great array of appetizers can help make the event. These recipes are easy to prepare and all taste amazing. You can even create a dinner from snacks, such as pairing my Ham and Cheese Sliders (page 29) and Roasted Carrot Hummus with Chile Crunch (page 46). Have fun with the ideas in this chapter, mix and match, and create the perfect spread for your friends.

ESSENTIALS: CHEESES, CHARCUTERIE, OLIVES, AND NUTS

As much as I love a cheese platter that is piled high with irresistible accompaniments, I also love simplicity. A cheese platter can be kept simple and still be a stunning presentation. Use only the best ingredients and the flavors of each item will shine through. I typically buy the finest-quality cheeses, charcuterie, and accompaniments my budget will allow, but purchase fewer items and in smaller amounts.

Here are a few ingredients I always have on hand for a quick cheese and charcuterie platter.

- Three or four different cheeses defined by age and texture, such as a firm aged cheese like Cheddar, a soft-ripened cheese like Brie, a semisoft cheese like Gouda, and a semihard cheese like Manchego. Try to pick a variety of milks—cow, goat, sheep—and distinctive flavors too.
- Assorted salami, such as Genoa, Napoli, and soppressata
- Castelvetrano olives
- Marcona almonds
- Honeycomb
- Crackers

HAM *and* CHEESE SLIDERS

SERVES 6

5 tablespoons unsalted butter

2 teaspoons minced
yellow onion

1 tablespoon Dijon mustard

2 teaspoons Worcestershire
sauce

2 teaspoons poppy seeds

1 package (12 count)
King's Hawaiian sweet rolls

½ lb ham, thinly sliced

½ lb Swiss cheese, thinly sliced

I've been making these classic sliders for years and everyone raves about them. They are the culinary hit of any gathering I host and are easy to make. The soft, fluffy King's Hawaiian rolls add just the right touch of sweetness and are widely available.

Preheat the oven to 350°F.

In a small saucepan over low heat, melt the butter with the onion. Add the mustard, Worcestershire sauce, and poppy seeds and stir until smooth. Remove from the heat.

Open each package of rolls and lay them on a work surface. Using a long serrated knife and a gentle sawing motion, split each "sheet" of rolls in half horizontally, keeping them the roll halves attached to one another. You will cut them into individual rolls after they are baked.

Lay the bottom halves of the rolls in a single layer in a 9 x 13-inch baking pan. Lay half of the ham slices evenly over the roll bottoms. Lay half of the cheese slices evenly over the ham. Top the cheese with the remaining ham slices followed by the remaining cheese slices. Place the roll tops over the layers of ham and cheese. Slowly and evenly pour the butter mixture over the top of the rolls, using a rubber spatula to spread an equal amount over each roll.

Bake the sliders until the cheese melts, about 20 minutes. Because every oven is different, check on the rolls after 15 minutes to see how much more time they need.

When the sliders are ready, cut around the rolls to separate them, then transfer to a platter. Serve warm.

WHIPPED RICOTTA CROSTINI
served three ways

SERVES 6

Sourdough Crostini (page 33)

FOR THE WHIPPED RICOTTA

2 cups whole-milk
ricotta cheese

4 oz cream cheese, at
room temperature

2 tablespoons olive oil

1 teaspoon grated lemon zest

½ teaspoon salt

**FOR THE STRAWBERRY-PEPPER
CROSTINI**

6 strawberries, hulled and
sliced lengthwise

1 teaspoon ground black pepper

**FOR THE PISTACHIO-RAISIN
CROSTINI**

¼ cup pistachios, shelled
and lightly crushed

¼ cup golden raisins

**FOR THE HONEY–ORANGE
ZEST CROSTINI**

Honey, for drizzling

3 teaspoons grated orange zest

Small edible fresh flowers,
for garnish

Sometimes I feel like I can devour a batch of this creamy whipped ricotta all by myself! It's perfect for making these beautiful crostini and for using as a dip with crackers, pita bread, or vegetables, and you can whip it up in just minutes.

Make the sourdough crostini as directed and set aside.

To make the whipped ricotta, in a bowl, using an electric mixer, beat the ricotta on medium speed until light and smooth. This can also be done in a high-powered blender. On low speed, add the cream cheese, oil, lemon zest, and salt and beat until fully incorporated. Raise the mixer speed to high and beat until creamy and smooth, about 1 minute If you can't get a smooth texture with the mixer, scoop the ricotta mixture into a blender and blend on high speed for 2 minutes. This always works! You should have about 2½ cups.

To assemble the crostini, spoon the whipped ricotta into a piping bag fitted with a small plain tip or into a ziplock bag and cut off the bottom corner. Pipe a cloud-like shape onto each crostino and then top about one-third of the ricotta-topped crostini with each suggested topping: strawberry slices sprinkled with the pepper; pistachios and raisins; and a drizzle of honey, a dusting of orange zest, and a flower garnish. Arrange the crostini on 1 or 2 platters and serve.

RECIPE CONTINUES

CONTINUED FROM PAGE 30

SOURDOUGH CROSTINI

1 sourdough baguette

½ cup olive oil

¼ teaspoon salt

MAKES ABOUT 30

Preheat the oven to 425°F.

Cut the baguette on the diagonal into slices ¼ to ½ inch thick. You should have about 30 slices. Lightly brush both sides of each slice with the oil, arranging them in a single layer directly on a large sheet pan as you work. Pour the salt into your hand, then lightly and evenly sprinkle the salt over all the slices.

Bake the slices until light golden brown, about 6 minutes. Then, using tongs, flip them over and bake until golden brown and crispy on the edges, 2–3 minutes longer. Remove from the oven and let cool.

To give the crostini a savory flavor, rub a garlic clove over the oil-brushed bread slices before you slide them into the oven. Baking times may vary slightly depending on your oven, so keep an eye on the crostini as they toast.

EDEN'S TIP: *You can top the crostini with the whipped ricotta, place the ingredients for the three toppings in small bowls, and invite your guests to assemble their own crostini. You can also serve the whipped ricotta on its own.*

MUSSELS *in* BUTTERY MISO BROTH

SERVES 4

1 lb mussels (about 24)

4 tablespoons unsalted butter, at room temperature

3 tablespoons white miso paste

1 tablespoon chopped fresh flat-leaf parsley

1 tablespoon chopped fresh thyme

¼ cup olive oil

4 cloves garlic, thinly sliced

½ teaspoon red pepper flakes

¼ cup water

Crusty bread, for serving

Trust me when I say this: you will want to drink this buttery broth! A breeze to make, this delectable appetizer is packed with flavor that will impress your guests. Serve with crusty bread for soaking up all the delicious liquid, or make a batch of the Sourdough Crostini (page 33) for serving alongside.

Place a large bowl in the sink and fill it with cool water. Put the mussels into the water to soak as you clean them. Using a stiff brush, scrub each mussel to remove any dirt or stringy bits adhering to the shell. Check for a beard (thin, fibrous tuft extending from the crack where the shells meet) and remove by either tugging on it to free it or by dislodging it with the brush. (Not every mussel will have a beard, as some beards will have been removed in processing.) Make sure each mussel is firmly closed. If a mussel is open, tap it gently against the rim of the bowl. If it does not slowly close tightly, discard the mussel. Also discard any mussels with cracked shells. Drain the mussels, rinse well, and set aside.

In a small bowl, mix together the butter and miso and set aside. On a small plate, mix together the parsley and thyme and set aside.

In a large pot over high heat, warm the oil with the garlic until the garlic turns golden brown, 2–3 minutes. This happens quickly, so keep an eye on the pot. Using a slotted spoon, transfer the garlic to the plate with the herbs.

Add the red pepper flakes to the oil and then add the mussels and cook, stirring, until the shells begin to open, about 1 minute. Add the water and the butter-miso mixture and cook, stirring, until all the mussels have opened and are coated with sauce, 1–2 minutes. Remove from the heat and remove and discard any mussels that failed to open.

Stir in the herbs and garlic and transfer to a serving bowl. Serve right away with crusty bread.

QUESO FUNDIDO
with KIELBASA

SERVES 4

5 tablespoons olive oil

13 oz kielbasa, cut into slices
½ inch thick

2 tablespoons chopped shallot

¼ cup tequila

1 can (4 oz) diced green chiles,
drained

1 jar (4 oz) diced pimentos,
drained

½ lb Monterey Jack cheese,
shredded

I combined three of my favorite things to make this dish: cheese, pimentos, and chiles. I like to serve it straight from the skillet, with a towel wrapped around the handle. The queso fundido pairs perfectly with the kielbasa, but you can also serve it with crostini (page 33).

In a large skillet over medium heat, warm 3 tablespoons of the oil. Add the kielbasa slices in a single layer and cook, turning once, until lightly browned on both sides, about 5 minutes on each side. Transfer to a plate and keep warm.

While the kielbasa cooks, place a medium skillet over low heat, add the remaining 2 tablespoons oil and the shallot, and cook, stirring occasionally, until the shallot is soft, about 5 minutes. Pour in the tequila, raise the heat to high, and cook until evaporated, about 30 seconds. Add the chiles and pimentos, stir well, then reduce the heat to low and stir in the cheese. Cook, stirring constantly, until the cheese melts, about 5 minutes. Remove from the heat.

Serve the queso fundido directly from the skillet or transfer to a fondue pot set over a heat source. Accompany with the warm kielbasa slices.

ORANGE BUTTERMILK DIP
with SEASONAL VEGETABLES

FOR THE DIP

½ cup sour cream

¼ cup buttermilk

1 teaspoon grated orange zest

¼ teaspoon salt

¼ teaspoon ground
black pepper

¼ teaspoon cayenne pepper

⅛ teaspoon ground nutmeg

2 tablespoons finely chopped
fresh chives

Fresh vegetables, for serving

There's nothing easier than mixing up than this vibrant, zesty, creamy dip and serving it alongside a platter of garden-fresh vegetables. Select three or four vegetables according to the season. Among my favorite choices are sugar snap peas, endive, cauliflower, radishes, and cucumbers.

To make the dip, in a bowl, whisk together the sour cream, buttermilk, orange zest, salt, black pepper, cayenne pepper, and nutmeg until smooth and creamy. You should have a scant 1 cup. Garnish with the chives.

Arrange the vegetables on a large platter or board, place the dip alongside, and serve.

FANCY HOMEMADE ONION DIP

SERVES 4

½ cup canola oil

½ cup minced yellow onion

½ teaspoon salt

½ teaspoon garlic powder

½ teaspoon onion powder

1 cup sour cream

2 tablespoons chopped fresh chives

Freshly ground black pepper

Small fresh edible flowers, for garnish (optional)

Potato chips, for serving

It's hard to remember a family gathering or holiday party without an onion dip. Paired with crunchy potato chips, this is one of those appetizers that pleases nearly everyone. Here I make the dip from scratch, which takes it up a notch—fancier without being complicated. To save time, prepare the dip the day before your get-together and store it in an airtight container in the fridge. If you're hosting a large gathering, whip up a double batch.

In a small skillet over medium-high heat, warm the oil. When the oil is hot, add the onion, salt, garlic powder, and onion powder and cook, stirring occasionally, until the onion is browned, about 10 minutes.

Remove from the heat and pour the contents of the skillet into a fine-mesh sieve, draining the onion well. Let the onion cool, then transfer to a bowl, add the sour cream, and stir to mix well.

To serve, garnish the dip with the chives, a sprinkle of pepper, and the flowers, if using, and serve the potato chips alongside.

EDEN'S TIP: *Always taste the dip to see if you prefer more salt. For a fancy dinner party, top it with caviar.*

CHARCUTERIE
served three ways

One rule of entertaining is always to have a snack out to eat when your company arrives. That way, if guests come very hungry, they can have something small to satisfy them before the meal. These three ideas for serving charcuterie are simple, easy to assemble, and will help curb your guests' hunger until dinner is ready.

LEMON-THYME BURRATA WITH SLICED SALAMI

For this platter, you'll need creamy burrata cheese, sliced salami, good-quality olive oil, finely chopped fresh thyme, grated lemon zest, Marcona almonds., and flaky sea salt. Arrange the burrata and sliced salami on a small platter. Sprinkle the thyme, lemon zest, and salt over the burrata, then drizzle with oil. Scatter the almonds around the platter.

TRUFFLE POTATO CHIPS WITH PROSCIUTTO

I once had this at a restaurant in Asheville, North Carolina, and I thought it was a fun idea for a quick appetizer. You'll need a 4-oz bag of truffle potato chips, 8 thin prosciutto slices, torn, and some freshly cracked black pepper. Stack the chips high on a plate or in a bowl and drape the prosciutto slices over the top. Finish with a few twists of pepper and serve.

PEACHES, BLUE CHEESE, AND PROSCIUTTO

I could eat this combination all day! (You can switch out the peaches for apples in the winter and spring.) All you need are perfectly ripe peaches, your favorite blue cheese, thinly sliced prosciutto, and crostini (page 33). Arrange the cut peaches, a good-size wedge of blue, and the prosciutto on a platter or board and set the crostini alongside. I like to add a drizzle of honey over the top of the peaches, blue cheese, and prosciutto. If you prefer a different cheese, a high-quality fresh mozzarella or a creamy Brie would be a good choice.

CAVIAR PLATTER

SERVES 4

1 sourdough or sweet baguette

½ cup sour cream

½ cup crème fraîche

¼ cup finely chopped red onion

2 tablespoons finely chopped fresh chives, plus whole chives for garnish

¼ cup finely chopped fresh dill, plus sprigs for garnish

1 bag (8 oz) potato chips

2–4 oz caviar

Caviar adds a touch of sophistication to any event and is an elegant yet straightforward luxury that can served with little effort. Offer it as an appetizer with such accompaniments as potato chips, toasted baguette slices, crème fraîche, and herbs. Or serve it for a charming cocktail party with your best Champagne.

First ready all the accompaniments. Slice and toast the baguette as directed for Sourdough Crostini (page 33). Put the sour cream, crème fraîche, onion, chives, and dill in separate small bowls and arrange the bowls on a large platter or board.

Fill as many bowls as you have containers of caviar with ice and set them on the platter.

Add the crostini and potato chips to the platter. Place dill sprigs and whole chives around the platter to add color. Lastly, remove the caviar from the refrigerator, uncover, and place on the ice. Set a mother-of-pearl spoon next to the caviar for guests to scoop out small amounts. Serve at once.

EDEN'S TIPS: *Serve caviar in its original container on a bed of ice to keep it cold while guests create their caviar appetizer.*

Use a mother-of-pearl spoon when serving caviar. A metal one will give the caviar an off-flavor. Or use any other non-metal spoon, such as tortoiseshell or animal horn.

It's imperative to keep the caviar refrigerated until just before serving, and don't let it remain at room temperature for more than 2 hours.

Caviar is expensive, so be sure to purchase it from a reputable source to guarantee you are serving a quality product.

ROASTED CARROT HUMMUS
with CHILE CRUNCH

FOR THE CARROTS

5 large carrots, peeled and cut into ½-inch-thick slices

2 cloves garlic, peeled

1 tablespoon olive oil

½ teaspoon salt

1 can (15 oz) chickpeas

½ cup tahini

¼ cup olive oil

3 tablespoons fresh lemon juice

1 tablespoon grated lemon zest

1 tablespoon ground ginger

1 teaspoon ground cumin

1 tablespoon seeded and chopped jalapeño chile

2 tablespoons chile crunch oil

EDEN'S TIP:
If you want a less spicy hummus, omit the chile crunch and garnish with 1 tablespoon finely chopped fresh chives and 1 tablespoon toasted sesame seeds (see Note, page 87).

A perfect recipe for *apéro* (French for that small bite before a meal), this riff on the popular Middle Eastern dip gets its beautiful orange color from roasted carrots and its little spicy kick from jalapeño chile. It can be served with pita bread, crackers, or raw vegetables for dipping.

To roast the carrots, preheat the oven to 425°F. Line a large sheet pan with parchment paper.

Arrange the carrot slices in a single layer on the prepared sheet pan. Tuck the garlic cloves in among the carrots, then drizzle the carrots evenly with the olive oil and sprinkle evenly with the salt.

Roast the carrots until tender when pierced with a knife tip, about 30 minutes. Remove from the oven and let cool for 5 minutes.

Open the can of chickpeas and drain the chickpeas into a sieve placed over a liquid measuring cup. You will need at least ½ cup chickpea liquid (you may need more for thinning the finished dip); add water if needed to equal that amount. In a blender, and working in batches if necessary, combine the chickpeas and chickpea liquid, tahini, oil, lemon juice and zest, ginger, cumin, jalapeño chile, and the roasted carrots and garlic cloves. Start the blender on low speed and gradually increase the speed, stopping the blender to scrape down the sides of the beaker as needed. Blend until the hummus is smooth and creamy, adding more chickpea liquid or some water if needed to achieve a good consistency.

Using a rubber spatula, scrape the hummus into a serving bowl. Drizzle the surface with the chile crunch and serve.

MARINATED GOAT CHEESE

1 log (8 oz) fresh goat cheese

½ cup olive oil, plus more
if needed

3 cloves garlic, smashed

3 lemon zest strips

2 fresh thyme sprigs

½ teaspoon red pepper flakes

Pinch of fresh oregano leaves

1 teaspoon fresh lemon juice

⅓ cup canola oil

This is one of my favorite appetizers with crackers, olives, and charcuterie. The combination of oils and seasonings infuses the cheese with incredible flavor.

Cut the goat cheese log into rounds ½ to 1 inch thick. Place a goat cheese round on the bottom of a 20-oz glass jar and drizzle the round with a bit of the olive oil. Top with 1 garlic clove and 1 lemon zest strip. Add 2 more goat cheese rounds, drizzle with more olive oil, and add 1 garlic clove, 1 lemon zest strip, 1 thyme sprig, and the red pepper flakes. Add the remaining cheese rounds, garlic clove, lemon zest strip, and thyme sprig; the oregano; the lemon juice; the remaining olive oil; and the canola oil. If the cheese is not covered by oil, add olive oil as needed just to cover. Cap the jar and marinate the mixture in the refrigerator overnight.

Remove the jar from the refrigerator 1 hour before serving so the oils can come to room temperature. Serve directly from the jar with a cheese knife or pour into a serving bowl.

YOGURT TAHINI DIP

2 cups whole-milk plain yogurt

¼ cup tahini

2 tablespoons fresh lemon juice

1 clove garlic, grated (use a citrus grater)

½ teaspoon salt

3 tablespoons olive oil

2 tablespoons chopped fresh chives

Flaky sea salt and freshly ground black pepper

Pita chips, pita bread, crackers, or crusty baguette, for serving

This is an all-around dip for crackers or pita bread. You will need to drain the yogurt at least overnight, so some planning is necessary. But this step is worth the effort, as it yields a thicker, creamier texture.

Place a medium-mesh sieve over a glass bowl. Spoon the yogurt into the sieve, cover with plastic wrap, and place in the refrigerator to drain at least overnight or for up to 2 days for a thicker texture.

Discard the liquid in the bowl, then add the drained yogurt to the same bowl. Add the tahini and stir until evenly incorporated. Then add the lemon juice, garlic, and salt and stir to mix well.

Transfer the dip to a shallow serving bowl and drizzle the oil over the top. Garnish with the chives, flaky salt, and pepper and serve with pita chips.

EDEN'S TIP: *The consistency of the yogurt will vary depending on the brand. It may need to drain longer than overnight to achieve a good result. To change things up, trade out the chives for another fresh herb, such as oregano or mint, or sprinkle the dip with a ground spice, such as cumin or sumac.*

POPCORN BAR

ROSEMARY + PARMESAN POPCORN

4 cups popped popcorn

2 tablespoons olive oil

1 tablespoon chopped fresh rosemary

¼ cup grated Parmesan cheese

STRAWBERRY POPCORN

4 cups popped popcorn

3 tablespoons strawberry powder

2 tablespoons popcorn oil or melted ghee

Melted white chocolate, for drizzling

BUFFALO POPCORN

4 cups popped popcorn

2 tablespoons popcorn oil or melted ghee

¼ cup buffalo hot sauce

Crumbled blue cheese, for sprinkling

EVERYTHING BAGEL POPCORN

4 cups popped popcorn

2 tablespoons popcorn oil or melted ghee

2–3 tablespoons everything bagel seasoning

There have been many times when I've sat around with friends and snacked on popcorn well into the evening, chatting about family and life. Popcorn, like cake and other desserts, makes me feel nostalgic, as it brings to mind exciting or fun moments in my life—from going to the movies to walking around at carnivals to decorating our Christmas tree. What better way to add a bit of nostalgic charm than to serve popcorn at your next gathering. The flavor possibilities, both sweet and savory, are countless, so there's something for everyone.

Each recipe will flavor 4 cups of popped popcorn (from 2 tablespoons of kernels).

MORE POPCORN FLAVOR IDEAS

· **Bacon and Chive Popcorn:** Toss a few cooked bacon slices, chopped, and finely chopped fresh chives.

· **Fried Jalapeño Popcorn:** Toss with chopped jalapeño chiles fried in oil.

· **Chile Crunch Popcorn:** Drizzle with chile crunch and toss well.

· **Candy Bar Popcorn:** Chop up your favorite candy bars and toss well.

· **Cacio e Pepe Popcorn:** Toss with melted ghee, freshly ground black pepper, flaky sea salt, and grated Parmesan cheese.

EDEN'S TIP: *Don't melt regular butter for tossing with the popped popcorn. The water content is too high, and it will shrink the popcorn and make it soggy. You can use a butter-flavored popcorn oil, or if you wish to use butter, try ghee, which is South Asian clarified butter. Look for it in jars in well-stocked supermarkets or in South Asian markets. Coconut oil or olive oil is also a good choice. Remember, less is more when it comes to dressing popcorn. Don't saturate it. Add just enough for the seasonings to stick.*

COMPOUND BUTTER
with CROSTINI

MAKES ABOUT 1 CUP

1 cup (2 sticks) unsalted butter, at room temperature

1 clove garlic, grated (use a citrus grater)

2 tablespoons chopped fresh chives

1 tablespoon chopped fresh rosemary, thyme, or sage

1 teaspoon small edible fresh flowers, such as pansies or borage

1 teaspoon grated lemon zest

¼ teaspoon salt

½ teaspoon ground black pepper

Sourdough Crostini (page 33), for serving

A compound butter adds charm and extra flavor when you are serving bread at your gathering. You can form the butter into a log, which is easy to slice, but I prefer fanciful shapes, as they look nicer and it's simple to do with inexpensive food-grade flexible silicone molds.

In a bowl, using an electric mixer, beat the butter on medium speed, stopping to scrape down the bowl sides as needed, until light and fluffy, about 5 minutes.

Add the garlic, chives, rosemary, flowers, lemon zest, salt, and pepper and, using a rubber spatula, mix until all the ingredients are evenly incorporated. Press the butter firmly into a mold and scrape the top of the mold clean. Cover and refrigerate overnight to harden.

When you're ready to serve the butter, pop it out of the mold and let it sit out for about 10 minutes to soften slightly, then serve alongside the sourdough crostini.

Simple Sides

Sides complete a meal. They complement the main dish and add color, texture, and more flavors to your menu. Choosing the best sides to accompany a main is all about balance. For example, a crisp corn salad (page 69) is perfect alongside my shredded pork tacos (page 83), and my cranberry-studded, orange-scented corn bread (page 62) is a great partner for barbecued ribs or other barbecued meats. I'm also a huge fan of pasta salads (page 65), which are nostalgic and a guaranteed crowd-pleaser. A simple platter of roasted vegetables is also always welcome. All of the sides here are easy to prepare and make the experience of gathering and eating together more enjoyable.

CHIVE *and* BLACK PEPPER DROP BISCUITS

MAKES 8 BISCUITS

2 cups all-purpose flour

1 tablespoon baking powder

2 teaspoons ground
black pepper

1 teaspoon salt

1 teaspoon sugar

¼ cup chopped fresh chives

¾ cup (1 ½ sticks) cold unsalted
butter, cut into cubes

¾ cup buttermilk, plus up to
2 tablespoons if needed

Drop biscuits are the easiest homemade biscuits you can make. They require very little work but yield a yummy flavor and texture. However, I feel they have to be eaten with whipped butter, and they taste even better if you serve them with my whipped compound butter (page 54).

Preheat the oven to 400°F. Line a sheet pan with parchment paper.

In a large bowl, stir together the flour, baking powder, pepper, salt, sugar, and chives, mixing well. Scatter the butter over the flour mixture and, using a pastry blender or 2 knives, cut in the butter until the mixture is the texture of a coarse meal with some pea-size pieces of butter mixed in.

Pour the buttermilk over the dry ingredients and, using a fork, stir and toss just until the dry ingredients are evenly moistened. Add up to 2 more tablespoons buttermilk if needed to moisten evenly, but stop before the dough gets too wet. Do not overmix the dough; it's good to have lumps.

Using a large trigger scoop or a large spoon, scoop 8 rough mounds (about ⅓ cup each) onto the prepared sheet pan, spacing them about 2 inches apart. Bake the biscuits until they are golden brown and a toothpick inserted into the center of a biscuit comes out with moist crumbs attached, 15–20 minutes. Serve warm or at room temperature.

ORANGE-CRANBERRY CORN BREAD *with* CARDAMOM

SERVES 10

½ cup (1 stick) unsalted butter, melted and cooled slightly cooled, plus room-temperature butter for the pan

1 cup dried cranberries

½ cup plus 2 tablespoons fresh orange juice

1 cup all-purpose flour

1 cup yellow cornmeal

2 teaspoons baking powder

½ teaspoon baking soda

2 teaspoons grated orange zest

1¼ teaspoons salt

1 teaspoon ground cardamom

2 large eggs

1½ cups sour cream

⅓ cup pure maple syrup

1 teaspoon pure vanilla extract

A good corn bread recipe is a must for entertaining! It can be served year-round with everything from chili, roasted chicken, and barbecued ribs to ham and turkey. This version is incredibly moist and packed with flavor, thanks to the orange and cranberries. I serve it with whipped orange-maple butter (see Eden's Tip), and leftover corn bread is delicious with coffee the next morning.

Preheat the oven to 350°F. Butter the bottom and sides of a 9- or 10-inch round springform pan.

In a small bowl, combine the cranberries and ½ cup of the orange juice and set aside to plump the cranberries. In a medium bowl, stir together the flour, cornmeal, baking powder, baking soda, orange zest, salt, and cardamom, mixing well. In a liquid measuring cup, stir together the eggs, sour cream, maple syrup, melted butter, vanilla, and the remaining 2 tablespoons orange juice, mixing well.

Pour the egg mixture into the flour mixture and, using a rubber spatula, gently fold together just until the dry ingredients are evenly moistened. Add the cranberries and their soaking liquid and fold just until evenly mixed. Don't overmix the batter.

Pour the batter into the prepared pan. Bake the corn bread until the top is golden brown and a toothpick inserted into the center comes out clean, about 30 minutes. Let cool in the pan on a wire rack for a few minutes, then unclasp and lift off the sides and ease off the bottom onto the rack. Serve warm.

EDEN'S TIP: *To make orange-maple butter, in a bowl, using an electric mixer on medium-high speed, beat ½ cup (1 stick) unsalted butter, at room temperature, until light and fluffy. Add 1 tablespoon grated orange zest and 2 tablespoons pure maple syrup and beat until well mixed. Press into a ramekin for serving.*

SESAME PASTA SLAW

SERVES 6

1 package (8 oz) macaroni pasta

1 package (14 oz) coleslaw mix

½ white onion, finely chopped

½ English cucumber, finely chopped

1 green bell pepper, seeded and finely chopped

¾ cup mayonnaise

½ cup buttermilk

¼ cup cider vinegar

2 tablespoons toasted sesame oil

2 tablespoons soy sauce

1 tablespoon sugar

1 teaspoon salt

½ teaspoon ground black pepper

¼ cup sesame seeds, toasted (see Note, page 87)

I can never stop eating this pasta salad, which is great any day of the year and is the perfect side for grilling day. Store-bought coleslaw mix makes it super easy to prepare, and if I am lucky enough to have some left over the next day, it tastes even better with shredded cooked chicken mixed in (see Eden's Tip). Serve the slaw at room temperature or chilled. It's delicious either way.

Bring a pot of salted water to a boil over high heat. Add the pasta and cook until al dente, according to the package directions. Drain well and let cool.

While the pasta is cooking, empty the coleslaw mix package onto a cutting board and chop into smaller pieces with a sharp knife. Ready the onion, cucumber, and bell pepper at the same time.

In a large bowl, combine the mayonnaise, buttermilk, vinegar, sesame oil, soy sauce, sugar, salt, and pepper and mix well to make the dressing. Add the cooled pasta, coleslaw mix, onion, cucumber, and bell pepper and stir until all the ingredients are evenly coated with the dressing.

Transfer to a serving bowl, sprinkle the sesame seeds over the top, and serve.

EDEN'S TIP: *Add some shredded cooked chicken—roasted at home or a rotisserie bird from the market—to the salad to turn this recipe into a main dish.*

LOIS'S BACON SALAD *with* WARM BACON VINAIGRETTE

SERVES 6

1 head red leaf lettuce, trimmed and chopped into bite-size pieces

1 head radicchio, trimmed and chopped into bite-size pieces

5 green onions, white and tender green parts, thinly sliced on the diagonal

9 slices thick-cut bacon, cut into 1-inch pieces

¼ cup sugar

½ cup cider vinegar

A friend passed this recipe along to me, and I have made it several times since because—I am warning you—the warm bacon vinaigrette is addicting! Once you have washed and dried the greens and fried the bacon, this salad comes together quickly and is perfect for serving anytime of the year.

Immerse the lettuce and radicchio in cold water to rinse well, then spin dry in a lettuce spinner. Transfer the greens to a serving bowl and add the green onions. Set aside.

In a skillet over medium heat, fry the bacon, stirring occasionally, until cooked through and crisp, about 10 minutes. Remove from the heat and, using a slotted spoon, transfer the bacon to a plate and set aside.

To make the dressing, you'll want about ¼ cup bacon fat in the pan. You don't need to measure it. Just eye what you have and remove and discard the excess or reserve for another use.

Turn the burner on to low heat, add the sugar and vinegar to the bacon fat, and heat, stirring occasionally, until the sugar has melted and the mixture is warm, 2–3 minutes.

Pour the warm dressing over the salad and toss to mix well. Top with the reserved bacon and serve at once.

EDEN'S TIP: *Add some grated pecorino romano cheese or diced avocado before pouring on the dressing. Serve this salad with roasted chicken or an easy pasta dish.*

CILANTRO-LIME CORN SALAD *with* COTIJA CHEESE

SERVES 4

4 ears corn, husks and
silks removed

2 radishes, finely chopped

¼ cup finely chopped
fresh cilantro

1 tablespoon seeded and finely
chopped jalapeño chile

2 tablespoons chopped
green onion, white and
tender green parts

1 clove garlic, pressed or minced

2 tablespoons olive oil

1 tablespoon grated lime zest

2 tablespoons fresh lime juice

¾ teaspoon salt

½ teaspoon ground black
pepper

2 oz Cotija cheese, crumbled
(about ½ cup)

Growing up in California, I was surrounded by the wonderful blend of flavors of two great traditions, California cooking and Mexican cooking. Mexican street corn was a favorite of mine, and this recipe is inspired by it. I like something light and fresh when I serve chips, meat, and cheese, and this corn salad fits the bill. It's bursting with flavor and has just the right amount of crunch. The salad is just right to serve alongside my pulled pork tacos (page 83).

Bring a pot of water to a boil over high heat. Add the corn and boil for 5 minutes. The kernels should be crisp tender. Using tongs, transfer the ears to a cutting board and let cool until they can be handled. One at a time, lay the cooled ears flat on the board and, using a large knife, slice the kernels off the first side, then rotate the ear cut side down and cut off the kernels from the next side. Repeat until all the kernels are removed. Transfer the kernels to a serving bowl.

Add the radishes, cilantro, chile, green onion, and garlic to the corn and toss to mix. Then add the oil, lime zest and juice, salt, and pepper and give everything a good stir.

Top with the crumbled Cotija and serve.

EDEN'S TIP: *Cotija is a mild, lightly salty Mexican cow's milk cheese named for a town in Michoacán. It is available in many well-stocked supermarkets, but if you cannot find it, grated pecorino romano cheese can be substituted.*

CHOPPED SALAD *with* CITRUS-CUMIN DRESSING

SERVES 6

FOR THE DRESSING

1 clove garlic, peeled

¼ teaspoon salt

3 tablespoons fresh lime juice

3 tablespoons fresh orange juice

2 teaspoons finely chopped shallot

1 tablespoon honey

1 teaspoon ground cumin

¼ cup olive oil

Freshly ground black pepper

FOR THE SALAD

3 ears corn, husks and silks removed

2 romaine hearts, trimmed and chopped into bite-size pieces

½ cup grated Parmesan cheese

5 green onions, white and tender green parts, thinly sliced

2 large avocados, halved, pitted, peeled, and diced

8 radishes, halved lengthwise and thinly sliced into half-moons

1 cup finely chopped fresh cilantro

2 cups roasted chickpeas (about 8 oz)

By now, you know that I love a beautiful presentation. Rows of colorful fresh vegetables make an attractive statement and the perfect side dish. This salad is excellent to serve throughout the year.

To make the dressing, on a cutting board, mince and mash the garlic with the salt to form a paste, then transfer to a small bowl. Add the lime juice, orange juice, shallot, honey, and cumin to the garlic-salt paste, then whisk together until well mixed. Slowly add the oil in a thin stream while whisking constantly until emulsified. Season with pepper, then taste and adjust the seasoning with more salt and honey if needed. Set the dressing aside.

To make the salad, bring a pot of water to a boil over high heat. Add the corn and boil for 5 minutes. The kernels should be crisp tender. Using tongs, transfer the ears to a cutting board and let cool until they can be handled. One at a time, lay the cooled ears flat on the board and, using a large knife, slice the kernels off the first side, then rotate the ear cut side down and cut off the kernels from the next side. Repeat until all the kernels are removed.

Put the romaine into a large serving bowl or a shallow platter. You will now arrange the remaining ingredients in rows on top of the romaine for the beautiful—and charming—presentation. The first row is the Parmesan cheese, followed by the green onions, corn kernels, avocados, radishes, cilantro, and finally the chickpeas. Your rows are now complete.

Just before serving, give the dressing a quick whisk and pour it over the top.

EDEN'S TIP: *I love the presentation of this salad on the table, but once I serve it, I like to toss all the ingredients with the dressing. You can swap out the crunchy chickpeas for toasted almonds or even for Doritos or other tortilla chips. Anything that adds a little crunch will work.*

MELON BAR *with* WHIPPED FETA

SERVES 8

FOR THE WHIPPED FETA

½ lb feta cheese

½ cup whole-milk plain yogurt

1 tablespoon grated lemon zest

2 tablespoons olive oil

½ teaspoon red pepper flakes

½ seedless watermelon

½ honeydew

½ cantaloupe

2 tablespoons chile lime salt

2 tablespoons Floral Finishing Salt (page 20)

2 tablespoons flaky sea salt

Small piece honeycomb

6 lemon wedges

The contrast between the sweet, juicy melon and the pleasant tang of the creamy whipped feta is a flavor explosion! Using different types of salt varieties adds depth to this colorful melon bar. The trio of ingredients is one of those combinations that you don't realize you like until you try it, and then it's just irresistible!

To make the whipped feta, in a food processor, combine the feta, yogurt, and lemon zest and process until smooth. With the processor running, slowly stream in the oil, then continue to process until smooth and creamy. Add the red pepper flakes and process until well mixed. You should have about ¾ cup. Scoop the whipped feta into a serving bowl.

To prepare the watermelon, honeydew, and cantaloupe, cut the melon halves in half, then cut the flesh away from the rind and discard the rind. Cut the melon flesh into small triangles, small cubes, or fun shapes and arrange them attractively on a large serving board.

Put each salt into its own small bowl and add to the board along with the bowl of whipped feta, the honeycomb, and the lemon wedges. Serve at once.

EDEN'S TIP: *Be creative and use melon in season and festive salt, which you can buy at your local grocery store or specialty food market. I sometimes cube the melons for a different look.*

Party Mains

As you already know, I will never suggest that you cook a five-course meal when you are having company. But these recipes are perfect if you want to make a main dish for guests. They are great no matter the season, call for ingredients easy to find at your local grocery store, and are simple to prepare. I have included a favorite cheesy baked pasta dish (page 79), foolproof tacos (page 83), and a fluffy broccoli quiche with a wonderful buttery crust (page 88), to name just a few of the highlights you'll find in the following pages.

RICOTTA-STUFFED PASTA SHELLS

SERVES 8

3 tablespoons unsalted butter

3 tablespoons olive oil

1 yellow onion, thinly sliced

1 clove garlic, minced

2 heads radicchio, trimmed and finely chopped

1 package (12 oz) jumbo pasta shells

2 cups whole-milk ricotta cheese

2 packages (7 oz each) Sartori Tuscan cheese blend (mixture of shaved Parmesan and shaved fontina cheese) (see Eden's Tip)

2 tablespoons chopped fresh flat-leaf parsley

2 tablespoons chopped fresh basil

2 large eggs, lightly beaten

½ teaspoon salt

½ teaspoon ground black pepper

½ teaspoon red pepper flakes

3 cups Rao's homemade marinara sauce or other high-quality jarred marinara sauce

½ cup heavy cream

I have been making this recipe, which I adapted from one I saw in *Food & Wine,* for over a decade, and it is always a hit with guests. Like so many of my dishes, it can be served year-round and pairs perfectly with a simple salad. I consider Rao's homemade marinara sauce the best jarred marinara on the market, and it is widely available.

In a large skillet over medium-low heat, melt the butter with the oil. Add the onion and garlic and cook, stirring occasionally, until lightly browned, about 10 minutes. Add the radicchio and cook, stirring occasionally, until fully wilted and very soft, about 10 minutes. Add a little water to the pan if the vegetables begin to scorch. Transfer the mixture to a large bowl and let cool.

Fill a large pot three-fourths full with salted water and bring to a boil over high heat. Add the pasta shells (you won't need the full package, just about 10 oz) and cook for about 2 minutes less than the time indicated on the package, as they will finish cooking in the oven. Drain into a colander and place under cool running water to cool completely. Then let drain for a few minutes to help dry them.

Meanwhile, make the filling: Fold the ricotta cheese, half of the cheese blend, the parsley, and the basil into the cooled vegetables, mixing well. Stir in the eggs, salt, black pepper, and red pepper flakes until fully incorporated. Set aside.

To make the sauce, in a large liquid measuring cup, stir together the marinara sauce and cream, mixing well. Pour 2 cups of the sauce mixture into a 9 x 13-inch baking dish.

RECIPE CONTINUES

CONTINUED FROM PAGE 79

Preheat the oven to 375°F.

One at a time, fill the pasta shells with 1–2 tablespoons of the cheese filling and nestle them in the sauce-lined baking dish, arranging them close together in a single layer. (Never stack them on top of one another or they will harden during baking.) If you cannot fit all of the stuffed shells in the dish, pour a little of the sauce mixture in a separate small baking dish and arrange the leftover shells in the dish.

Pour the remaining sauce mixture evenly over the shells, covering them if you can. Top the shells with the remaining cheese blend, distributing it evenly.

Bake uncovered until the sauce is bubbling and the top is golden brown, 30–40 minutes. Let rest for 10 minutes before serving.

EDEN'S TIP: *If you cannot find the Sartori Tuscan cheese blend at your local market, it's easy to create your own blend. Using a cheese shaver, a vegetable peeler, or the wide slots on a box grater, shave 7 oz each Parmesan cheese and fontina cheese.*

To save time, make the filling the day before your party; cover and refrigerate it until you are ready to stuff the shells.

SLOW COOKER PORK TACOS *and* TACO BAR

SERVES 8

FOR THE PORK

5 lb boneless pork shoulder

½ cup sugar

¼ cup salt

¼ cup olive oil

1 yellow onion, cut into quarters

3 cloves garlic, smashed

5 orange zest strips, removed with a vegetable peeler or paring knife

FOR THE TACO BAR

16–20 corn tortillas, warmed

Pickled jalapeño chiles and carrots

Chopped fresh cilantro

Diced avocado

Chopped onion

Sour cream

Pico de gallo or other salsa

Sliced limes

EDEN'S TIP: *This pork is also good on mini King Hawaiian rolls. You can also cook the pork in a covered baking dish or roasting pan in a preheated 300°F oven, about 40 minutes per pound.*

These tacos are one of my favorite meals to make when hosting a small gathering. Fixing the pork is so straightforward! First, it marinates in the refrigerator overnight with sugar and salt, which makes it incredibly juicy and flavorful. Then it spends hours in a slow cooker, where the meat breaks down and becomes super tender. I serve the pork with warm tortillas and an array of toppings and let guests assemble their own tacos.

To make the pork, put the pork shoulder into a large bowl. Rub the pork with the sugar and salt, covering every surface. Wrap the pork in plastic wrap, leave it in the bowl, and let rest in the refrigerator overnight.

The next day, unwrap the pork and brush off the excess sugar and salt. Place a large skillet over medium-high heat and pour in the oil. When the oil is hot, add the pork and sear, turning as needed, until golden brown and crispy on all sides, about 5 minutes on each side.

Transfer the pork to a slow cooker and add the onion, garlic, and orange zest strips, distributing them evenly around the pork. Cover and cook on low until the pork is super tender, juicy, and pulls apart easily with a fork, 10–12 hours.

Transfer the pork to a shallow bowl and, using 2 forks, pull it apart into shreds. Using a large spoon, skim the fat from the juices in the slow cooker, then spoon some of the juices over the pork to moisten it. Cover to keep warm if not serving immediately.

Just before the pork is ready, set up your taco bar: Have the warmed tortillas ready, wrapped in a napkin or kitchen towel. Set out toppings in small bowls next to the tortillas and pork.

YEAR-ROUND HERBY LEMON PASTA

SERVES 4-6

¾ cup olive oil

1 tablespoon grated lemon zest

½ cup fresh lemon juice

1 clove garlic, grated (use a citrus grater)

½ teaspoon salt

½ teaspoon ground black pepper

1 teaspoon red pepper flakes

1 lb linguine pasta

½ cup grated Parmesan cheese

½ cup chopped mixed fresh herbs, such as basil, flat-leaf parsley, chives, and dill

This versatile pasta can be served as a main or a side dish for any season or any holiday. It can also be altered to suit your taste, such as adding more garlic or different herbs or using a different type of pasta. It's a recipe our family enjoys often.

Fill a large pot three-fourths full with salted water and bring to a boil over high heat.

While the water heats, in a small bowl, combine the oil, lemon zest and juice, garlic, salt, black pepper, and red pepper flakes and stir well. You can make this mixture the day before, cover and refrigerate it, and then bring it to room temperature before using.

When the water is at a boil, add the linguine and cook until al dente, according to the package directions. Test a strand to be sure it is ready. Scoop out a little of the pasta water and set aside, then drain the pasta and transfer it to a serving bowl.

Give the oil-lemon mixture a quick stir, then pour it over the pasta and toss to coat the noodles evenly. Add the cheese and herbs and gently toss again, adding a little of the reserved pasta water if needed to help the sauce cling to the linguine. Serve at once.

EDEN'S TIP: *I like to use naturally colored linguine for a fun touch.*

PEANUT BUTTER NOODLES
with SHREDDED CHICKEN

½ lb linguine pasta

6 tablespoons toasted
sesame oil

6 tablespoons creamy
peanut butter

¼ cup soy sauce

1 tablespoon red wine vinegar

1 tablespoon firmly packed
light brown sugar

3 cloves garlic, minced

1 tablespoon olive oil

1 cup roughly chopped
broccolini

1 cup shredded roasted chicken
breast (store-bought roast
chicken is fine)

¼ cup sesame seeds, toasted

4 green onions, white and
tender green parts, thinly sliced
on the diagonal

EDEN'S TIP:
*This pasta is great
because it can be
served lukewarm or
at room temperature.
Switch out the
broccolini if you prefer
a different vegetable.*

This sounds like an odd combination, but I promise, if you like peanut butter and toasted sesame seeds, this pasta is for you. One of the best things about the dish is that it can be served at room temperature, and when you're hosting, that is a godsend.

Fill a pot three-fourths full with salted water and bring to a boil over high heat. Add the linguine and cook until al dente, according to the package directions.

While the water heats and the pasta cooks, in a bowl large enough to hold the pasta, whisk together the sesame oil, peanut butter, soy sauce, vinegar, sugar, and garlic, mixing well. Set aside.

In a small saucepan over medium heat, warm the olive oil. Add the broccolini and cook, stirring, for 2–3 minutes. Then cover and cook, stirring once or twice to prevent scorching, just until tender, about 4 minutes longer. Remove from the heat and set aside.

When the pasta is ready, drain the pasta, add to the bowl with the peanut butter sauce, and stir until the noodles are evenly coated with the sauce. Add the broccolini and chicken and stir and toss to mix well.

Transfer the dressed noodles to a serving bowl. Top with the sesame seeds and green onions and serve.

Note: *To toast the sesame seeds, pour them into a skillet over medium heat and toast, stirring occasionally, until golden brown and fragrant, 3–5 minutes. Watch closely as they can burn easily. Immediately pour onto a plate to cool.*

BROCCOLI QUICHE *with* HOMEMADE BUTTERY CRUST

This quiche can be served for any meal. The filling has a light, fluffy texture, and the Jarlsberg cheese gives it a distinctive nutty flavor. The crust, flaky and buttery, is my go-to recipe for all pies and quiches. If pressed for time, use a good-quality store-bought crust.

SERVES 4–6

FOR THE CRUST

2½ cups all-purpose flour, plus more for dusting

1 tablespoon sugar

1 teaspoon salt

1 cup (2 sticks) cold unsalted butter, cut into cubes

¼ cup cold vegetable shortening, such as Crisco

5 tablespoons ice water, plus more if needed

FOR THE FILLING

1½ cups chopped broccoli

1½ cups shredded Jarlsberg cheese

½ cup shaved Parmesan cheese

4 large eggs

1 cup heavy cream

½ small yellow onion, grated (use the small holes on a box grater)

½ teaspoon salt

¼ teaspoon ground black pepper

⅛ teaspoon ground nutmeg

1 large egg, lightly beaten, for egg wash

To make the crust, in a large bowl, stir together the flour, sugar, and salt, mixing well. Scatter the butter over the top and, using a pastry blender or your fingers, work in the butter until it is the size of peas. Add the shortening and work it in with your fingers until the mixture is the consistency of coarse crumbs. Do not overmix. The mixture should be dry and powdery. Sprinkle with the ice water and mix it in with your fingers until the dough holds together when pinched and comes together in a loose, rough ball. If the dough crumbles, add a little more ice water.

Transfer the dough to a lightly floured work surface and pat it into a thick disk. Wrap in plastic wrap and refrigerate for 30 minutes. Roll out the dough into a 12-inch round about ½ inch thick. Roll the dough around the rolling pin and position the pin over a 10-inch deep-dish pie dish. Unroll the dough and center it in the dish, gently pressing it into the bottom and up the sides. Using a small knife or kitchen scissors, trim the dough, leaving a 1-inch overhang. Roll the overhang under itself to create a high edge, then pinch the dough to form a fluted edge. Freeze the crust for 30 minutes. Preheat the oven to 350°F.

To make the filling, half fill a skillet with water and bring to a boil over high heat. Add the broccoli, reduce the heat to medium, cover, and cook until crisp tender, 3–5 minutes. Drain and set aside.

In a large bowl, whisk together 1 cup of the Jarlsberg, the Parmesan, eggs, cream, onion, salt, pepper, and nutmeg, mixing well. Fold in the broccoli.

Remove the crust from the freezer and pour the filling into it. Sprinkle the remaining ½ cup Jarlsberg over the top. Brush the edge of the crust with the egg wash. Bake the quiche until the filling is just set and the top is golden brown, 40–45 minutes. Transfer to a wire rack and let cool before serving.

VODKA BAKED RIGATONI *with* ITALIAN SAUSAGE MEATBALLS

SERVES 6–8

1 lb rigatoni pasta

2 tablespoons unsalted butter

¼ cup olive oil

2 cups finely chopped yellow onion

3 cloves garlic, minced

½ cup vodka

1 can (28 oz) crushed plum tomatoes, with juice

1 can (14 oz) tomato sauce

1¼ cups heavy cream

2 fresh thyme sprigs

2 teaspoons dried oregano

1 teaspoon salt

1 teaspoon ground black pepper

½ teaspoon red pepper flakes

½ lb sweet Italian pork sausage, casings removed

1½ cups grated Parmesan cheese

EDEN'S TIP:
To save time, make the sauce a day before the party and store in an airtight container in the refrigerator.

You can't have enough baked pasta recipes when entertaining! Call me old-school, but these are my staples when having company over. This one is great because it has meatballs without making them. Genius, right?

Fill a large pot three-fourths full with salted water and bring to a boil over high heat. Add the rigatoni and cook for about 5 minutes less than the time indicated on the package, as the pasta will finish cooking in the oven. Drain the pasta and pour it into a 9 x 13-inch baking dish.

While the water heats and the pasta cooks, make the sauce: In a large saucepan over medium heat, melt the butter with the oil. Add the onion and cook, stirring occasionally, until softened, about 5 minutes. Add the garlic and stir to mix, then pour in the vodka and cook until all the liquid nearly evaporates, about 3 minutes. Add the crushed tomatoes and their juice, tomato sauce, cream, thyme sprigs, oregano, salt, black pepper, and red pepper flakes and stir well. Simmer, stirring occasionally, until the sauce thickens and the flavors blend, about 20 minutes.

While the sauce simmers, preheat the oven to 375°F. Using your palms, roll the sausage into ½-inch balls and set aside.

Pour the sauce over the cooked pasta, scatter the meatballs over the top, then toss everything gently to coat the pasta with the sauce and distribute the meatballs evenly. Sprinkle the cheese evenly over the top.

Bake uncovered until the pasta is al dente, the sauce is bubbling, and the top is lightly browned, 25–30 minutes. Remove from the oven and let sit for 5 minutes before serving.

CREAMY PEA PASTA
with CRISPY PROSCIUTTO

EDEN'S TIP: *Always taste the sauce and, little by little, add what you feel it needs. If it needs more salt, add a pinch. If it needs a stronger lemon accent, grate in a little more zest. Tasting is vital.*

To change it up, trade out the prosciutto for pancetta or bacon.

Even before they take their first bite, your guests will be sold on this luscious pasta because of its vibrant color. The sauce takes just 5 minutes to make in a blender—so easy and so delicious!

Preheat the oven to 400°F. Line a sheet pan with parchment paper and lay the prosciutto slices in a single layer on the parchment.

Bake the prosciutto until crispy, about 10 minutes. Let cool, then break into small pieces with your hands and set the pieces aside.

Meanwhile, fill a large pot three-fourths full with salted water and bring to a boil over high heat. Add the pasta and cook until al dente, according to the package directions.

While the water heats and the pasta cooks, make the sauce: In a blender, combine the basil, spinach, peas, garlic, shallot, pine nuts, Parmesan, lemon zest, and salt and pulse until all the ingredients are finely chopped. With the blender running on high speed, stream in the oil and then continue to blend on high speed until the mixture is smooth.

When the pasta is ready, scoop out ¼ cup of the pasta water and set aside, then drain the pasta and transfer it to a bowl. Add the sauce and the reserved pasta water to the pasta and mix together until the pasta is evenly coated with the smooth, silky sauce.

Transfer the pasta to a serving bowl, sprinkle with the crispy prosciutto, and serve.

SOUTHERN CHEESE
and CHARCUTERIE BOARD

¾ lb smoked sausage, such as andouille

¾ lb kielbasa

¾ lb smoked turkey sausage

¼ cup olive oil

½ lb American cheese

½ lb sharp Cheddar cheese

½ lb jalapeño Cheddar cheese

1 cup pimento cheese (about 8 oz; homemade or store-bought)

½ lb green olives

½ lb pepperoncini

½ cup barbecue sauce

½ cup spicy mustard

½ cup hot honey

½ lb pickled okra

24 saltine crackers

Paprika, for sprinkling

From California to East Tennessee! We lived in the South for a few years, and it was a wonderful experience for our family and our bellies. Southern food is delicious, y'all! One of my favorite takeaways from those days was the Southern cheese platter. Not long after we arrived, our neighbors fixed us one, and we devoured it. A unique twist on a classic cheese and charcuterie board, this is a little heartier so it can be a meal. I love the flavors of barbecue sauce, seared sausages, and spicy pickles all coming together on this popular Southern tradition.

Cut all the sausages into slices ½ inch thick. In a large cast-iron skillet over medium heat, warm the oil. Working in batches if needed to avoid crowding, add the sausage slices in a single layer and pan-fry, turning once or twice, until heated through and nicely browned on both sides, 6–7 minutes. Transfer to a board or platter when ready to serve.

Cut the American, Cheddar, and jalapeño cheeses into slices ¼ inch thick. Scoop the pimento cheese into a small bowl.

Put the olives, pepperoncini, barbecue sauce, mustard, and honey in individual small bowls and place on a large serving board or platter. Add all the sausages and cheeses, the pickled okra, and the crackers to the board or platter, arranging them attractively around the bowls. Sprinkle paprika over all the sausages and cheeses for extra flavor and color and then serve.

> EDEN'S TIP: *Instead of cooking the sliced sausages on the stove top, you can fire up your grill and grill the links over a medium fire, turning as needed to avoid burning, until heated through and browned and a bit crispy on the outside, 6–8 minutes. Transfer to a cutting board and cut into ½-inch-thick slices for serving.*

Every Party Needs Dessert

I am a dessert girl through and through. It's the only way to end a weekend meal and is nonnegotiable whenever I entertain. I've compiled some of my favorite dessert recipes in this chapter, such as my chocolate espresso cupcakes (page 123) and the best chocolate chip cookies (page 107) you'll ever eat. I've also included ideas for desserts that you can assemble from store-bought items, such as ice cream sandwiches and a vintage candy board (see below).

THREE ASSEMBLED DESSERTS FOR ANY GATHERING

No time to bake? These come together quickly and are crowd-pleasers.

Ice Cream Soda Float

Switch up the traditional ice cream float by pairing healthier sodas with your favorite ice creams. You'll find many naturally flavored sodas with a low sugar content on the market today, in flavors ranging from berry to hibiscus to ginger and more. I love fruity combos, such as blackberry ice cream with strawberry basil soda.

Ice Cream Cookie Sandwich

Use store-bought cookies and ice cream to make easy and delicious ice cream cookie sandwiches. Prepare them ahead of time and keep them in the freezer until serving. A fun tip: Buy the ice cream in half-pint paper containers, then use a large, heavy knife to cut straight through the container, slicing it into ½-inch-thick slices. Peel away the paper from each slice, which fits perfectly between two large cookies.

Vintage Candy Board

A vintage candy board is a hit with any age at a gathering. Kids love it, and seeing and tasting candy from childhood is nostalgic for adults. Try to include a variety of types, such as gummies, chocolates, fruit-flavored hard candies, and caramels You can customize this idea to any holiday or party theme. For example, around Easter, lots of traditional candies are available at markets, specialty stores, and online, making assembling your candy board easy and fun.

SHORTBREAD CRUMBLE BARS *with* FRUIT PRESERVES

MAKES 9 BARS

1½ cups (3 sticks) unsalted butter, at room temperature

4 oz cream cheese, at room temperature

1 cup granulated sugar

1 teaspoon pure vanilla extract

1 teaspoon grated orange zest

3 cups all-purpose flour

1 teaspoon baking powder

¼ teaspoon salt

1½ cups fruit preserves, any type

FOR THE GLAZE

4 oz cream cheese, at room temperature

1 cup confectioners' sugar

2 tablespoons whole milk, plus more if needed

½ teaspoon grated orange zest

EDEN'S TIP: *These bars can be made up to 2 days in advance and stored in an airtight container in the refrigerator. Serve at room temperature.*

Quick and easy to make, these butter-delicious shortbread bars are topped with a luscious cream cheese glaze. You can use any flavor of fruit preserves you like. I especially like lemon, blueberry, raspberry, and apricot. For smaller servings, cut the shortbread into 12 squares.

Preheat the oven to 350°F.

In a food processor, combine the butter, cream cheese, and granulated sugar and process until smooth and creamy. Add the vanilla and orange zest and process until well mixed. In a bowl, stir together the flour, baking powder, and salt, mixing well. Add the flour mixture to the processor and pulse just until the mixture forms a crumbly, evenly moist dough.

Gather the dough into a rough ball and divide the ball in half. Wrap half in plastic wrap and refrigerate. Place the remaining half in a 9-inch square baking pan and press firmly and evenly onto the bottom of the pan.

Bake the dough for 15 minutes. It will be soft to the touch and pale. Remove from the oven and spread the preserves evenly over the top. Remove the remaining dough from the refrigerator and crumble it over the preserves.

Return the pan to the oven and bake the shortbread until the top is golden brown, about 25 minutes. Transfer to a wire rack and let cool completely.

While the shortbread cools, make the glaze: In a bowl, using an electric mixer, beat together the cream cheese, confectioners' sugar, milk, and orange zest on high speed until smooth. It should be the consistency of hot fudge. If it is too thick, add a little more milk.

Using a spoon, drizzle the glaze evenly over the shortbread, then let stand until the glaze sets, about 10 minutes. Then, using a sharp knife, cut the shortbread into 9 equal squares and carefully remove them from the pan to serve.

COCONUT BUNDT CAKE

SERVES 8

FOR THE CAKE

1 cup (2 sticks) unsalted butter, at room temperature, plus more for the pan

1½ cups all-purpose flour, plus about ¼ cup for the pan

1 teaspoon salt

½ teaspoon baking powder

1½ cups granulated sugar

3 large eggs, at room temperature

½ teaspoon pure vanilla extract

½ teaspoon pure almond extract

½ cup unsweetened canned coconut milk

1 cup sweetened shredded dried coconut

FOR THE COCONUT GLAZE

1 cup confectioners' sugar

⅓ cup unsweetened canned coconut milk

1 teaspoon pure vanilla extract

Sweetened shredded dried coconut, for garnish

> **EDEN'S TIP:** *Make sure you heavily butter every crevice of the Bundt pan and dust with a light layer of flour to ensure the cake releases. This is a crucial step when making this cake.*

This cake has been a staple in our house and in the homes of *Sugar and Charm* readers for years. It has a wonderfully moist texture and the perfect amount of buttery sweetness. It is a great go-to dessert year-round, from a springtime luncheon to a backyard gathering on a summer evening to a winter holiday table.

To make the cake, preheat the oven to 350°F. Butter a 10-inch Bundt pan, using a small piece of paper towel to make sure you grease every crevice well. Don't be shy with the butter! When the entire pan is well greased, add the ¼ cup flour and twirl, shake, and tilt the pan so the flour coats the butter evenly, especially any areas where there is a design. Flip the pan upside down and tap lightly to release any excess flour. Greasing and flouring the pan well is important to ensure the cake easily unmolds after baking.

In a medium bowl, stir together the flour, salt, and baking powder, mixing well; set aside. In a large bowl, using an electric mixer, beat together the butter and granulated sugar on medium speed until light and fluffy, about 3 minutes. Add the eggs one at a time, beating after each addition just until incorporated. Beat in the vanilla and almond extracts until incorporated. Turn off the mixer and scrape down the sides of the bowl with a rubber spatula.

On low speed, add the flour mixture in three additions alternately with the coconut milk in two additions, beginning and ending with the flour mixture and beating after each addition just until incorporated. This step should take about 2 minutes total. Turn off the mixer. Using the rubber spatula, scrape down the sides of the bowl and along the bottom to make sure all the ingredients are evenly mixed. Then, still using the spatula, fold the shredded coconut into the batter.

Pour the batter into the prepared Bundt pan. Bake the cake until the top is a nice golden brown and a toothpick inserted near the center comes out clean, about 1 hour. The timing can be a little shorter or a little longer depending on

RECIPE CONTINUES

CONTINUED FROM PAGE 103

your oven, so set the timer for 45–50 minutes and begin checking from that point. Let the cake cool completely in the pan on a wire rack.

While the cake cools, make the glaze: In a medium bowl, whisk together the confectioners' sugar, coconut milk, and vanilla until smooth and glossy.

Invert the cooled cake onto a serving plate and lift off the pan. Pour the glaze over the cake, allowing it to drip down the sides. Top with a little more shredded coconut for fun. Let the glaze set for about 5 minutes before serving.

EDEN'S TIP: *If the top is browning too much before the cake is ready, lay a piece of aluminum foil over the top to prevent more browning.*

I like using the toothpick method to test this Bundt cake for doneness. If the cake is removed from the oven too early, it will sink in the middle.

COCONUT OIL CHOCOLATE CHIP COOKIES

MAKES 20

2½ cups all-purpose flour

1 teaspoon baking soda

½ teaspoon baking powder

½ teaspoon salt

¾ cup coconut oil (it's fine if it's semisolid)

1¼ cups firmly packed dark brown sugar

½ cup granulated sugar

2 large eggs

1 teaspoon pure vanilla extract

1 teaspoon pure almond extract

2 cups semisweet chocolate chips

EDEN'S TIP: *If you do not have coconut oil, you can substitute canola oil.*

The dough can be made up to 2 days in advance and stored in an airtight container in the refrigerator until you're ready to bake.

This is a take on the most popular cookie recipe on *Sugar and Charm*—my butter-free chocolate chip cookies. Here, I have traded out the vegetable oil for coconut oil and to my surprise, the result is incredible. This is now my favorite chocolate chip cookie recipe by far.

Preheat the oven to 350°F. Line a large sheet pan with parchment paper.

In a medium bowl, stir together the flour, baking soda, baking powder, and salt; set aside. In a large bowl, using an electric mixer, beat together the coconut oil, brown sugar, and granulated sugar on medium speed until smooth and creamy. Add the eggs one at a time, beating after each addition just until incorporated. Add the vanilla and almond extracts and beat just until incorporated.

On low speed, add the flour mixture in three additions, beating after each addition just until incorporated. Using a rubber spatula, fold in the chocolate chips until evenly distributed.

Using a 2-inch cookie scoop or a large spoon, drop mounds of the dough onto the prepared sheet pan, spacing them 2 inches apart so they have room to spread as they bake. You should have 20–22 cookies.

Bake the cookies until lightly golden, 10–12 minutes. Be careful not to overbake these cookies. They should be gooey when you take them out of the oven, and they will continue to cook as they cool. Let cool on the pan on a wire rack for at least 5 minutes before serving. They are delicious warm or at room temperature.

Store leftover cookies in an airtight container at room temperature for a few days or in the freezer for up to 3 months.

BANANA PUDDING TRIFLES *with* FLUFFY MARSHMALLOW TOPPING

SERVES 8

1½ cups heavy cream

8 oz cream cheese, at room temperature

1 can (14 fl oz) sweetened condensed milk

2 cups cold 2-percent milk

1 package (5 oz) instant vanilla pudding mix (see Eden's Tip)

2 teaspoons pure vanilla extract

FOR THE MARSHMALLOW FLUFF

3 large egg whites, at room temperature

1 teaspoon cream of tartar

⅔ cup plus 1 tablespoon sugar

¾ cup light corn syrup

⅓ cup water

2 teaspoons pure vanilla extract

2 ripe bananas

1 package (5 oz) shortbread cookies

Here, I layer creamy vanilla pudding with shortbread cookies and sliced bananas, then top everything with homemade marshmallow fluff. This recipe has a few steps, but I've been making it for years and it's worth the time. The marshmallow fluff is the perfect topping for these trifles and is great on other desserts too, such as ice cream, cupcakes, and pies. But if you are short on time, sweetened whipped cream is a fine substitute.

First, make the whipped cream you will later fold into the pudding: In a stand mixer fitted with the whip attachment, beat 1 cup of the cream on high speed until stiff peaks form. Scoop the cream into a bowl and set aside. Rinse the mixer bowl.

Next, make sure the cream cheese is fully softened to room temperature. If it is not, unwrap it, place it on a microwave-safe plate, and microwave on high power for 15–20 seconds. Transfer the cream cheese to the mixer bowl, fit the mixer with the paddle attachment, and beat on high speed until light, fluffy, and lump-free. Add the condensed milk, 2-percent milk, the remaining ½ cup cream, the pudding mix, and vanilla and beat until completely smooth. The mixture will be somewhat thin now, but as it sits, it will thicken to a good pudding consistency.

Finally, using a rubber spatula, gently fold in the whipped cream just until evenly incorporated. Transfer to a bowl, cover, and refrigerate until you're ready to assemble the trifles.

RECIPE CONTINUES

CONTINUED FROM PAGE 108

EDEN'S TIP: *To save time on party day, make the pudding and the marshmallow fluff the day before and refrigerate them. When you're ready to finish the trifles, give the pudding a good stir and then start assembling. You can turn this into a single large trifle too.*

To make the marshmallow fluff, wash and dry the mixer bowl and whip attachment. Put the egg whites, cream of tartar, and 1 tablespoon of the sugar into the bowl and fit the mixer with the whip attachment. Beat on medium speed until foamy, then increase the speed to medium-high and beat until stiff, glossy peaks form. Turn off the mixer.

While the egg whites are whipping, in a deep, heavy saucepan over medium heat, combine the remaining ⅔ cup sugar, the corn syrup, and water and bring to a boil, stirring to dissolve the sugar. Then continue to boil, without stirring, until the mixture thickens, is a light golden color, and registers 240°F (soft ball stage) on a candy thermometer, 5–7 minutes. Letting the mixture boil this long is crucial for making a good fluff. If you need more time to reach the desired temperature, give it another minute or two. More time is better than less. When the syrup is ready, remove from the heat.

With the mixer on medium-low speed, slowly pour the syrup into the whites in a thin, steady stream, aiming it between the side of the bowl and the whip attachment. Make sure the syrup is mixing thoroughly with the egg whites, halting the pouring briefly if needed. Once the egg whites and syrup are combined, add the vanilla and beat until incorporated.

Now, gradually increase the mixer speed to high and beat until the mixture is thick, fluffy, shiny, and holds soft peaks, 5–10 minutes. Cover and refrigerate until needed.

To assemble the trifles, spoon the marshmallow fluff into a piping bag fitted with a small, plain tip or with a small hole cut at the bottom. Peel and slice the bananas. Break up the cookies a little. Remove the pudding from the refrigerator.

Line up 8 half-pint canning jars or other individual clear glass serving vessels. Spoon a layer of pudding into the bottom of each jar, top with some cookie pieces, and follow with a few banana slices. Repeat the layers until the jars are filled.

Pipe a nice crown of marshmallow fluff on top of each serving and, using a kitchen torch, lightly toast it. Serve at once.

SPRINKLE CAKE *with* SWISS MERINGUE BUTTERCREAM

SERVES 12–14

FOR THE CAKE

1 cup (2 sticks) unsalted butter, at room temperature, plus more for the pans

2½ cups all-purpose flour

1 tablespoon baking powder

1 teaspoon salt

1 cup whole milk

½ cup vegetable oil, such as canola oil

2 teaspoons pure vanilla extract

1 teaspoon pure almond extract

1½ cups sugar

4 large egg whites, at room temperature

1 large egg, at room temperature

½ cup colorful sprinkles

FOR THE MERINGUE BUTTERCREAM

1 cup sugar

4 large egg whites

1½ cups (3 sticks) unsalted butter, at room temperature

1 teaspoon pure vanilla extract

¼ cup colorful sprinkles, for garnish

This is my classic go-to birthday cake. Everything about it screams party, and it's a foolproof recipe I've been preparing for years. The frosting, which is a buttercream made with a light Swiss meringue and without confectioners' sugar, is also a favorite.

To make the cake, preheat the oven to 350°F. Butter the bottom and sides of two 8-inch round cake pans, then line the bottom of each pan with parchment paper.

In a medium bowl, stir together the flour, baking powder, and salt, mixing well. In a liquid measuring cup or a bowl with a spout, combine the milk, oil, and vanilla and almond extracts and stir together with a fork. Set both mixtures aside.

In a large bowl, using an electric mixer, beat together the butter and sugar on medium speed until light and fluffy, about 3 minutes. Add the egg whites one at a time, beating after each addition just until incorporated, then add the whole egg and beat just until incorporated. Turn off the mixer and scrape down the sides on the bowl with a rubber spatula.

On low speed, add the flour mixture in three additions alternately with the milk mixture in two additions, beating after each addition just until combined. Turn off the mixer. Using the rubber spatula, scrape down the sides of the bowl and along the bottom to make sure all the ingredients are evenly mixed. Then, still using the spatula, fold the sprinkles into the batter just until evenly distributed.

Divide the batter evenly between the prepared pans. Bake the cake layers until a toothpick inserted into the center comes out clean, 25–30 minutes. The timing will vary depending on your cake pans, oven, and location, so begin checking a little before 25 minutes has passed. Let cool in the pans on wire racks.

RECIPE CONTINUES

CONTINUED FROM PAGE 112

To make the buttercream, fill a saucepan with water to a depth of about 2 inches and bring to a simmer. Select a heatproof bowl that will rest snugly in the rim of the saucepan over (not touching) the water, add the sugar and egg whites to the bowl, and whisk together. Fit the bowl in the rim of the pan and whisk the sugar–egg white mixture constantly until the sugar is fully dissolved and the mixture is hot and frothy on top, about 5 minutes. The mixture should look like shiny marshmallow crème. This step is crucial, so use an instant-read thermometer to check the temperature. It should be 160°F.

Remove the bowl from the saucepan. Using a stand mixer fitted with the whip attachment, or a bowl and a handheld mixer, beat the egg white mixture on medium speed until cooled and thickened with glossy peaks, about 5 minutes. Add 1 stick of room-temperature butter at a time, beating after each addition until smooth.

On low speed, add the vanilla and beat until incorporated. If the buttercream curdles or separates, beat on high speed until it comes back together. Beat for 5–10 minutes, or however long it needs to become a smooth, light, and airy buttercream.

To assemble the cake, invert the cooled cake layers onto the wire racks, lift off the pans, and peel off the parchment. Place a cake layer on a round serving platter. Top it with a large dollop of the buttercream and, using an offset spatula, spread the buttercream evenly to the edges. Top with the second cake layer and spread the remaining buttercream over the top and the sides of the cake, if desired. Garnish with the sprinkles.

PEANUT BUTTER
RICE KRISPIE TREATS

½ cup (1 stick) salted butter, plus room-temperature butter for the baking pan

½ teaspoon pure vanilla extract

12 oz marshmallows

6 oz Rice Krispies (see Eden's Tip)

½ cup creamy peanut butter

FOR THE CHOCOLATE ICING

1 cup dark chocolate chips

5 tablespoons unsalted butter

2 tablespoons creamy peanut butter

1 teaspoon pure vanilla extract

¼ teaspoon salt

EDEN'S TIP: *Do not use a measuring cup to measure the Rice Krispies; weigh them on a scale. The most common-size box of Rice Krispies is 12 oz, so check your box and if that is what you have, you'll use just half. Double this recipe for a large gathering.*

Gooey, peanut buttery, brown buttery—these treats are so good, you will make them repeatedly. Make sure to serve them with napkins because they can get messy—in the best kind of way!

Butter the bottom and sides of a 9-inch square baking pan.

In a large, heavy saucepan over medium heat, melt the butter. Once it has melted, watch it closely and stir it occasionally. It is ready when it has turned golden brown, has a nutty aroma, and tiny brown specks are visible on the bottom of the pan. Watch carefully as it can go from brown to burned quickly. This browning process is essential for these treats to have a great flavor.

Reduce the heat to low and stir in the vanilla. Add the marshmallows and turn them with a wooden spoon to coat evenly with the brown butter. As you stir, the marshmallows will begin to melt. Continue to stir until the mixture is the consistency of marshmallow crème, about 3 minutes.

Remove from the heat, add the Rice Krispies, and stir until they are coated with the marshmallow mixture. Add the peanut butter and fold in just until all the ingredients are evenly mixed.

Pour the mixture into the prepared pan and spread it evenly with a rubber spatula. Cover the surface with a piece of parchment paper and press down on the parchment to create an even layer in the pan. Let sit for 30 minutes while you make the chocolate icing.

To make the icing, in a small, heavy saucepan over low heat, melt together the chocolate chips and butter, stirring occasionally. This will take just a few minutes. When the chocolate is almost melted, remove from the heat and stir to melt the remaining chips with the butter, stirring until smooth. Add the peanut butter, vanilla, and salt and stir until well mixed and smooth.

Remove the parchment, then pour the icing evenly over the mixture. Refrigerate for 10 minutes to set the chocolate, then cut into squares to serve.

NO-BAKE MASCARPONE CHEESECAKE

SERVES 10–12

FOR THE GRAHAM CRACKER CRUST

14 whole sheets (4 crackers each) graham crackers

6 tablespoons unsalted butter, melted and cooled

1 large egg yolk, lightly beaten

2 tablespoons granulated sugar

½ teaspoon salt

FOR THE FILLING

½ cup granulated sugar

8 oz cream cheese, at room temperature

2 tablespoons grated orange zest

½ teaspoon salt

1½ cups cold heavy cream

2 tablespoons confectioners' sugar

1 tub (8 oz) mascarpone cheese

2 teaspoons pure vanilla extract

EDEN'S TIP: *I like to leave the cheesecake on the bottom of the pan and serve it from there. That way, you won't have to move it around too much.*

A no-bake cheesecake? Yes, please! Technically, it's not "no bake" if you make the graham cracker crust (highly recommended), but you can use a premade crust if you like. The filling is deliciously creamy and liberally flecked with orange zest.

To make the crust, preheat the oven to 350°F. Break up the graham cracker sheets and drop them into a food processor. Pulse until finely ground (the texture of coarse sand). Measure 2 cups crumbs and transfer them to a bowl. (Any leftover crumbs can be saved for sprinkling over ice cream or pudding.)

Add the melted butter, egg yolk, granulated sugar, and salt to the crumbs and stir with a fork until well mixed and the crumbs are evenly moistened. Pour the crust mixture into a 9- or 10-inch springform pan. Using a flat-bottomed measuring cup, gently press the crumb mixture evenly into the bottom of the pan. The crust will be relatively thick.

Bake the crust until it is set and has taken on a little color, about 10 minutes. Let cool completely on a wire rack while you make the filling.

To make the filling, in a bowl, using a handheld mixer, beat together the granulated sugar and cream cheese on high speed until smooth and light in texture, about 3 minutes. Add the orange zest and salt and beat until incorporated. Set aside.

In a stand mixer, combine the heavy cream and confectioners' sugar and beat on medium-high speed until stiff peaks form. On low speed, add the mascarpone and vanilla and beat until well mixed. Remove the bowl from the mixer stand and, using a rubber spatula, gently fold the cream cheese mixture into the mascarpone mixture just until thoroughly mixed. The texture will be light and fluffy.

Scoop the filling into the cooled crust, spreading it evenly and smoothing the top. Cover and refrigerate for at least 8 hours or up to overnight. If the filling has not fully set, place the cheesecake in the freezer for 30 minutes. When ready to serve, unclasp and lift off the pan sides. Garnish the cheesecake and serve.

CHOCOLATE CHERRY CHUNK COOKIES

MAKES ABOUT 24 COOKIES

1 cup all-purpose flour

½ teaspoon baking soda

½ teaspoon salt

¾ cup (1½ sticks) unsalted butter, at room temperature

½ cup granulated sugar

½ cup firmly packed dark brown sugar

1 large egg

1 teaspoon pure vanilla extract

½ teaspoon pure almond extract

1 cup old-fashioned rolled oats

1½ cups semisweet chocolate chips or chunks

1½ cups dried tart cherries

½ cup pecans, chopped

These have been my favorite cookies for more than a decade. The recipe was given to me by my mother-in-law, who has been baking them for over thirty years. They have the yummiest flavor, and their texture is the best combination of crunchy and chewy. These are great to make ahead and freeze and then take out an hour before serving. I even love to eat them straight out of the freezer!

Preheat the oven to 350°F. Line a large sheet pan with parchment paper.

In a medium bowl, sift together the flour, baking soda, and salt; set aside. In a large bowl, using an electric mixer, beat together the butter, granulated sugar, and brown sugar on medium speed until smooth and fluffy, about 3 minutes. Add the egg and vanilla and almond extracts and beat until incorporated. Turn off the mixer and scrape down the sides of the bowl with a rubber spatula.

On low speed, slowly add the flour mixture and beat just until incorporated. Turn off the mixer and, using the rubber spatula, scrape down the sides and along the bottom of the bowl. Add the oats, chocolate chips, cherries, and pecans and beat on low speed until all the ingredients are evenly incorporated.

Using a 2-inch cookie scoop or a large spoon, drop mounds of the dough onto the prepared sheet pan, spacing them 2 inches apart so they have room to spread as they bake. You should have about 24 cookies.

Bake the cookies until golden brown, 12–14 minutes. Let cool on the pan on a wire rack for 1–2 minutes, then transfer the cookies to the rack. Serve warm or at room temperature. Store leftover cookies in an airtight container at room temperature for a few days or in the freezer for up to 3 months.

CHOCOLATE ESPRESSO CUPCAKES *with* ESPRESSO BUTTERCREAM

MAKES 24 CUPCAKES

FOR THE CUPCAKES

2 cups granulated sugar

1¾ cups all-purpose flour

¾ cup unsweetened cocoa powder (I use Hershey's)

2 teaspoons instant espresso powder

1½ teaspoons baking soda

1½ teaspoons baking powder

1 teaspoon salt

2 large eggs

1 cup whole or 2-percent milk

¾ cup vegetable oil or canola oil

2 teaspoons pure vanilla extract

1 cup boiling water

FOR THE ESPRESSO BUTTERCREAM

1 cup (2 sticks) unsalted butter, at room temperature

2 cups confectioners' sugar

2 tablespoons instant espresso powder

1 tablespoon whole or 2-percent milk

1 teaspoon pure vanilla extract

24 small edible flowers or chocolate-covered espresso beans

I am a chocolate girl through and through! I love a decadent chocolate dessert, and these cupcakes fit that description perfectly. Plus, the addition of espresso powder to both the cupcakes and the buttercream makes these gems especially lovely.

To make the cupcakes, preheat the oven to 350°F. Line two 12-cup standard muffin pans with paper liners.

In the bowl of a stand mixer, whisk together the granulated sugar, flour, cocoa powder, espresso powder, baking soda, baking powder, and salt, mixing well. In a liquid measuring cup, whisk together the eggs, milk, oil, and vanilla. Fit the mixer with the paddle attachment. On low speed, slowly add the egg mixture to the flour mixture and beat until fully mixed, stopping the mixer now and again to scrape down the sides and along the bottom of the bowl with a rubber spatula. Increase the mixer speed to medium and beat for about 30 seconds. Then turn down the speed to low and slowly add the boiling water. The batter will be quite liquid, and that's how you want it to be.

Spoon the batter into the prepared muffin cups of 1 muffin pan, filling each cup about half full and using half of the batter. Bake the cupcakes until they have risen in the center and are set to the touch, about 15 minutes. Let cool completely in the pan on a wire rack.

While the first pan of cupcakes is baking, fill the prepared cups of the second muffin pan with the remaining batter the same way. When the first pan of cupcakes is removed from the oven, slide the second pan into the oven and bake the same way, then remove from the oven and let cool.

RECIPE CONTINUES

CONTINUED FROM PAGE 123

While the cupcakes are cooling, make the buttercream: Using the clean bowl of the stand mixer fitted with the clean paddle attachment, beat the butter on high speed until light and fluffy, about 2 minutes. Turn off the mixer and add the confectioners' sugar. Then turn on the mixer to low and beat until the mixture is smooth. Add the espresso powder, milk, and vanilla and beat until incorporated. Turn off the mixer again and scrape down the sides and along the bottom of the bowl with the rubber spatula. Then turn on the mixer to high and beat until light and fluffy, about 4 minutes.

To frost the cupcakes, remove the cooled cupcakes from the pans. Using a large cookie scoop, add a dollop of the buttercream to the top of each cupcake. Then, using a small spoon, make a swirl or a slight indentation in the top of each dollop. This is the easiest way to frost a cupcake. Top each dollop with a flower and serve.

BROWN SUGAR–ROSEMARY SHORTBREAD COOKIES

MAKES 18-24
COOKIES

1½ cups all-purpose flour,
plus more for dusting

¼ cup cornstarch

½ teaspoon baking powder

½ teaspoon salt

1 cup (2 sticks) unsalted butter,
at room temperature

½ cup firmly packed
dark brown sugar

1¼ teaspoons chopped
fresh rosemary

½ teaspoon pure vanilla extract

Confectioners' sugar,
for dusting

The rosemary in my garden grows year-round, and I love using it in my recipes. Here, it adds a wonderful earthy flavor to buttery, crumbly, lightly sweetened shortbread cookies. You can cut these cookies into nearly any shape you like, from hearts to squares to stars, and they can be made in advance, giving you more time with friends on party day.

In a medium bowl, sift together the flour, cornstarch, baking powder, and salt; set aside. In a large bowl, using an electric mixer, beat the butter on medium speed until light and fluffy, about 3 minutes. Add the brown sugar and continue to beat until well mixed and fluffy, about 4 minutes. Add the rosemary and vanilla and beat until incorporated.

On low speed, slowly add the flour mixture and beat just until combined, stopping the mixer to scrape down the sides and along the bottom of the bowl with a rubber spatula as needed. Do not overmix. The dough will be sticky and soft. Turn the dough out onto a sheet of plastic wrap, shape into a thick disk, wrap well, and refrigerate for 1 hour.

Preheat the oven to 325°F. Line a large sheet pan with parchment paper.

Lay a large sheet of parchment paper on a work surface and dust lightly with a mixture of equal parts flour and confectioners' sugar. Unwrap the dough, place it on the center of the parchment, and dust the top with confectioners' sugar. Roll out the dough ¼ inch thick. Using one or more cookie cutters in any shape you like (1½- to 2-inch cutters are a good size), cut out as many cookies as possible and transfer them to the prepared sheet pan, spacing them about 1 inch apart. Gather up the dough scraps, press together, dust with confectioners' sugar, roll out, cut out more cookies, and add them to the pan.

Bake the cookies until pale golden brown, 15–17 minutes. Let cool on the pan on a wire rack for about 5 minutes, then transfer to the rack and let cool completely. They will keep in an airtight container at room temperature for up to 7 days, in the refrigerator for up to 10 days, or in the freezer for up to 3 months.

SUPER-SIMPLE BUTTERMILK ICE

SERVES 4-6

2½ cups buttermilk

1 cup heavy cream

1¼ cups sugar

1 tablespoon grated lemon zest

2 tablespoons fresh lemon juice

1 vanilla bean, split lengthwise

Small fresh thyme sprigs or grated lemon zest, for garnish

This dessert packs a lot of flavor! It is light and refreshing and is great to serve after a large meal. Plus, you don't need an ice-cream maker to prepare it.

In a bowl, combine the buttermilk, cream, sugar, and lemon zest and juice. Using the tip of a paring knife, scrape the seeds from the vanilla bean and add them to the bowl. Then whisk together all the ingredients until well mixed and the sugar has dissolved.

Pour the mixture into a freezer-safe dish or pan. I like to use a 9 x 5-inch loaf pan, which works perfectly. Freeze overnight.

The next day, just before serving, use a fork to break up the frozen mixture, scraping it until it forms what looks like thick shaved ice. Scoop into small individual bowls, garnish each serving with a small thyme sprig for extra color, and serve at once.

CHOCOLATE POPCORN BARK

SERVES 6-8

12 oz semisweet chocolate, chopped

½ cup popped popcorn

1 tablespoon dried edible flowers (dried blue lotus flowers, roughly chopped, are a good choice)

1 teaspoon flaky sea salt

2 tablespoons chopped nuts, such as pecans, walnuts, or peanuts

You can trade out the semisweet chocolate for dark or milk chocolate in this easy recipe, and for a double-chocolate treat, drizzle white chocolate over the top. The nuts can be varied too, depending on what you like or have on hand.

Line a sheet pan with parchment paper.

Put the chocolate into a heatproof bowl or the top pan of a double boiler. Fill a saucepan or the bottom part of the double boiler with water to a depth of about 1½ inches and bring to a simmer. Place the bowl or pan with the chocolate on top, making sure it is not touching the water. Heat the chocolate, stirring often, until melted and smooth. Alternatively, put the chocolate into a microwave-safe bowl and microwave in 15-second intervals, stopping and stirring after each interval, until melted and smooth.

Pour the chocolate onto the prepared sheet pan and, using an offset spatula or the back of a spoon, spread evenly about ¼ inch thick. It doesn't need to be a perfect shape or perfectly smooth. Top with the popcorn and flowers, distributing them evenly across the top, then sprinkle evenly with the salt and nuts.

Place the pan in the refrigerator until the chocolate has hardened, about 1 hour. Then break it into small pieces and enjoy!

COFFEE MILKSHAKE

SERVES 2

2 cups coffee ice cream,
plus more if needed, softened
for 5 minutes

1 cup whole milk, plus more
if needed

2 teaspoons instant espresso
powder

2 chocolate chip cookies,
for lids

The second job I ever had was at a little drive-up coffee shop in the remote town where I grew up. I loved being a barista, and I worked there until my move to Los Angeles. At the coffee shop, we made Kona coffee shakes, which called for coffee ice cream and espresso, and it quickly became one of my favorite treats. Fast-forward two decades later and this is now my son's favorite shake.

In a blender, combine the ice cream, milk, and espresso powder and blend until smooth and thick. If the shake is too thick, blend in a little more milk. If it is too thin, blend in a little more ice cream.

Pour into tall glasses, top with a cookie lid, and push the straw through the cookie. Serve at once.

ALMOND SNACKING CAKE *with* BERRIES

SERVES 8

¾ cup (1½ sticks) unsalted butter, at room temperature, plus more for the pan

2 cups superfine almond flour

⅓ cup all-purpose flour

1 teaspoon baking powder

1 teaspoon kosher salt

1 cup granulated sugar

3 large eggs, at room temperature

2 tablespoons grated lemon zest

1 tablespoon fresh lemon juice

2 teaspoons pure vanilla extract

1 cup blueberries and/or blackberries, plus more for serving

Confectioners' sugar, for dusting (optional)

Whipped crème fraîche, whipped cream, or ice cream, for serving

This is one of those cakes that pairs well with everything. You can use different types of berries according to the season, and it is wonderful served with whipped crème fraîche, whipped cream, or ice cream.

Preheat the oven to 350°F. Butter the bottom and sides of a 9-inch round cake pan.

In a medium bowl, stir together the almond flour, all-purpose flour, baking powder, and salt; set aside. In a large bowl, using an electric mixer, beat together the butter and granulated sugar on medium speed until light and fluffy, about 3 minutes. Add the eggs one at a time, beating after each addition just until incorporated. Add the lemon zest and juice and vanilla and beat until well mixed. The mixture might look curdled, but that is okay. On low speed, slowly add the flour mixture and beat just until combined, stopping the mixer to scrape down the sides and along the bottom of the bowl with a rubber spatula as needed. Do not overmix. Using the rubber spatula, fold in the berries.

Pour the batter into the prepared pan. Bake the cake until the top is puffed up in the center and golden brown and a toothpick inserted into the center comes out clean, about 30 minutes. Let cool completely in the pan on a wire rack, then run a small knife along the inside edge of the pan to loosen the cake and invert the cake onto the rack.

This cake is so yummy that it doesn't need frosting. If you like, dust the top with confectioners' sugar. Cut into slices and accompany each serving with a dollop of whipped crème fraîche and a spoonful of berries.

Pour Me a Drink

Nothing sets the mood like a festive drink! Come Friday, it's time for a cocktail, and if I'm hosting, I'll have one in a guest's hand before that person can say hi. Being greeted with a cocktail is something that never gets old.

I developed most of the drinks—both alcoholic and nonalcoholic—in this chapter to serve four to six guests. You can double them up and make extras to store in the refrigerator for easy refills. Once you've mixed up a batch of cocktails, it is important to sample it to make sure it is properly balanced. Use a small spoon to scoop up a taste and decide if more sweetness, alcohol, or citrus is needed. Use these recipes as a guide and add to them or riff on them as you like.

STOCKING THE BAR

Here is my guide to the bar tools and ingredients you'll need to make most of the cocktail recipes in this book. It's nice to have a well-stocked bar even when just a few friends gather. That way, you can whip up something delicious on a whim.

As with all types of ingredients, the quality of the spirits you stock makes a difference. Luckily, scores of boutique brands offer excellent quality for reasonable prices. I can get lost in a liquor store checking out all the gorgeous labels and spirits!

BAR TOOLS

- Cocktail shaker and strainer
- Jigger
- Muddler
- Barspoon
- Ice cube trays with large, square molds
- Paring knife
- Vegetable peeler
- Citrus reamer
- Wine opener and bottle opener

SPIRITS

Bitters: Made by infusing alcohol with botanicals, bitters are used to add a hint of bitterness and flavor to cocktails. I always have orange bitters, Angostura bitters, and aromatic bitters on hand.

Contratto Aperitif: I love to use this lovely red Italian-made aperitif for spritz cocktails and white sangria. It has a hint of orange flavor and is similar to Aperol, though less sweet. It's currently my go-to aperitif for a year-round spritz!

Dry vermouth: Indispensable for martinis, dry vermouth is a fortified wine infused with herbs and spices that's also good served over ice with a twist.

Elderflower liqueur: The floral flavor of this liqueur is perfect for quickly elevating prosecco or Champagne. I use it in my Floral Sangria (page 171), and I sometimes add a splash to a Garden Gin and Tonic (page 168) or even to plain soda water.

Gin: One of my favorite spirits, gin has a botanical flavor that makes for an excellent cocktail. I like to stock a purple gin (made by adding butterfly pea blossoms at the end of distillation) for preparing colorful cocktails, plus a clear gin for mixing a traditional gin and tonic and my Fizzy Cucumber Gimlet (page 149).

Rum: This spirit is essential for two cocktail-hour favorites, the mojito and the daiquiri, as well as for tropical drinks like the piña colada and the mai tai. I use rum in my Frozen Mojito (page 160) and Champagne Party Punch (page 163). Have a light and dark rum on hand.

Simple syrup: I don't keep this in my bar, but I always have some in the fridge. To make simple syrup, combine equal parts sugar and water in a small saucepan and bring to a simmer over medium heat, stirring constantly until the sugar fully dissolves. Remove from the heat, let cool, and store in a tightly capped container in the refrigerator, where it will keep for up to 4 weeks. You can also make the syrup with honey or brown sugar in place of the granulated sugar, or you can add herbs or berries to the pan while you are dissolving the sugar for a flavored syrup and then strain the syrup once it cools.

Tequila: Have a blanco and a reposado tequila on hand to make different versions of margaritas and other tequila-based cocktails.

Triple sec: This orange-flavored liqueur adds a hint of sweetness and citrusy flavor to such traditional cocktails as the margarita, the cosmopolitan, and the sidecar.

Vodka: This is an excellent base for many drinks, such as my Lemon Drop (page 155), Mango Mule (page 172), and Fizzy Blackberry-Ginger Smash (page 149).

Whiskey: A must-have for the Habanero Whiskey Sour (page 159), whiskey is also used in a classic old-fashioned.

MIXOLOGY CHEAT SHEET

If a friend stops by unexpectedly and you want to whip up a quick cocktail (which is pretty impressive), I'm here to give you the perfect formula to make any drink!

Put all of the following ingredients into a cocktail shaker. Double the amounts if you're making two drinks.

INGREDIENTS

**2 OUNCES
SPIRIT**

**1 OUNCE
SIMPLE SYRUP**

**1 OUNCE
FRESHLY SQUEEZED
CITRUS JUICE**

EDEN'S TIP: *Feel free to muddle fresh herbs in the cocktail shaker with the sweetener and citrus before adding the spirits and ice. Shake it all together and strain into a glass. You can also add herbs and botanicals by making infused simple syrups.*

1. **POUR IN A SPIRIT (2 OUNCES)**
   Gin, vodka, tequila, bourbon, or rum

2. **CHOOSE A SIMPLE SYRUP (1 OUNCE)**
   Make garden-infused syrups with herbs, fruits, and even veggies you grow! (See page 141.) Some fun flavors are mint, lavender, jalapeño, rosemary, and cucumber.

3. **ADD FRESH CITRUS JUICE (1 OUNCE)**
   Lime, lemon, grapefruit, or orange

4. **SHAKE WITH ICE FOR 20 SECONDS**
   Pour into a glass topped with ice and garnish with an edible flower.

COCKTAIL HERBS

Using fresh herbs in cocktails adds a unique and sophisticated flavor to your drinks. They not only look beautiful as garnishes but also help you create complex aromas and tastes. You can infuse your simple syrup with them, you can muddle them to add layers of flavors, or you can use them to garnish drinks.

I love my herb garden, which has saved me multiple times when I've run out of fresh herbs for the bar—and for the kitchen. It's worth growing a few herbs at home that you can use when entertaining. Here are the herbs I use the most when making cocktails.

MINT

LAVENDER

THYME

BASIL

ROSEMARY

TARRAGON

CILANTRO

SAGE

DILL

GUIDE TO SERVING WINE

SERVING TEMPERATURE

Serving wine at the correct temperature is essential to enjoying your drinking experience. Generally, the lighter the wine, the cooler you should drink it.

Temperature to Serve

Reds: 55°–65°F

Whites: 49°–55°F

QUICK CHILL

If you have forgotten to chill your wine in advance, wrap the bottle in a wet paper towel and bury it in the freezer for 5 to 10 minutes.

THE PROPER FILL

If serving still wine, pour 5 to 6 ounces into a glass. Always fill a glass only partway. Never fill it to the rim. If serving sparkling wine, offer it first, before any still wine, and pour 3 to 4 ounces into each flute.

Help guests keep track of their wineglasses by supplying them with a wine charm (decoration that fits around the stem of the glass), so if they set their glass down and walk away, they can find it again.

STORING OPENED WINE

Once a wine bottle has been opened, store it in the refrigerator. White wines will keep for two to five days and red wines will keep for three to five days.

PURCHASING WINE

Although the number of glasses you serve to each guest will depend on the length and nature of your party, in general, pouring two to three glasses per person for a casual gathering is recommended. A standard bottle of wine (750 ml) contains five servings, so shop with these amounts in mind. Also, it's a good idea to use a wine app to keep track of your favorite labels. It simplifies shopping.

DECANTING

Decanting wine primarily does two things: it separates any sediment from the liquid, and it aerates the wine. The latter allows the wine to breathe, which enhances its flavor and aroma. This practice particularly benefits older red wines, but it should also be done with young reds to ensure they reach their fullest potential.

WINE BY THE SEASON

Spring: Light reds, rosés, whites, and bubbles

Summer: Whites, rosés, and bubbles

Fall: Full-bodied whites, light reds, and bubbles

Winter: Full-bodied reds, rosés, and bubbles

FIZZY PITCHER DRINKS

FOR FIZZY BLACKBERRY-
GINGER SMASH

1 cup blackberries

3-inch slice fresh ginger, peeled
and cut into large pieces

4 oz fresh lemon juice

8 oz vodka

8 oz ginger beer

Fresh fruit, such as blackberries
or lemon wedges, for garnish

Candied or crystallized ginger,
for garnish

FOR FIZZY ORANGE-BASIL
MARGARITA

1 cup fresh basil leaves,
plus more for garnish

8 oz fresh orange juice

2 oz agave nectar

6 oz fresh lime juice

8 oz reposado tequila

3 oz triple sec or other
orange liqueur

8 oz lime or orange
sparkling water

Fresh or dehydrated orange
slices, for garnish

FOR FIZZY CUCUMBER GIMLET

10 cucumber slices, peeled or
unpeeled, plus more for garnish

4 oz simple syrup (page 141)

5 oz fresh lime juice

8 oz gin

8 oz lime sparkling water

I live for an easy pitcher cocktail recipe, as it lessens the stress on the bartender. These three recipes can be altered to suit your tastes—less alcohol or more sweetness is up to you. Plus, they are grand additions to gatherings year-round.

FIZZY BLACKBERRY-GINGER SMASH

In a pitcher, combine the blackberries, ginger, and lemon juice and muddle together until the berries and ginger are smashed. Pour in the vodka and ginger beer and stir to mix well.

Fill the pitcher with ice, garnish with fresh fruit and candied ginger, and serve at once.

FIZZY ORANGE-BASIL MARGARITA

In a pitcher, combine the basil, orange juice, agave nectar, and lime juice and muddle together until the basil is smashed. Pour in the tequila, orange liqueur, and sparkling water and stir to mix well.

Fill the pitcher with ice, garnish with an orange slice and basil leaves, and serve at once.

FIZZY CUCUMBER GIMLET

In a pitcher, combine the cucumber, simple syrup, and lime juice and muddle together until the cucumber is smashed. Pour in the gin and sparkling water and stir to mix well.

Fill the pitcher with ice, garnish with cucumber slices, and serve at once.

Fizzy Orange-Basil Margarita • page 149

Fizzy Cucumber Gimlet • page 149

PROSECCO SLUSHY POPS
with STRAWBERRY *and* PEACH

SERVES 6

10 oz frozen peaches

5 oz frozen strawberries

2 tablespoons fresh lemon juice

½ cup simple syrup (page 141)

2 cups prosecco

¼ cup vodka

3 large fresh mint leaves

Let's "pop" the cork for this fun and fruity treat that combines luscious fruit and bubbly prosecco! Whether hosting a pool party or enjoying a cozy night indoors, these slushy pops are guaranteed to be a hit. They come together quickly and are made the day before, so serving them couldn't be easier!

In a blender, combine the peaches, strawberries, lemon juice, simple syrup, prosecco, vodka, and mint and blend on high speed until smooth.

Let the mixture sit for 5 minutes to allow the bubbles to subside.

Pour the mixture into disposable ice-pop pouches and freeze for 24 hours. Serve the slushy pops in the pouches directly from the freezer.

LEMON DROP

SERVES 4

8 oz vodka

4 oz fresh lemon juice

3 oz simple syrup (page 141)

4 thin lemon slices, for garnish

4 edible flowers, for garnish

Invented in San Francisco in the 1970s, a classic lemon drop is one of my favorite drinks because it's light, refreshing, and includes just three simple ingredients. Those qualities also make it great for a gathering. Served in a beautiful coupe and garnished with a thin lemon slice and a fresh flower, this sweet and lemony vodka cocktail will be the star of the party.

In a cocktail shaker, combine the vodka, lemon juice, and simple syrup. Fill the shaker with ice, cover, and shake vigorously for at least 30 seconds to blend and chill the ingredients.

Strain evenly into 4 small coupes or martini glasses. Garnish each cocktail with a lemon slice and a flower and serve at once.

CILANTRO MARGARITA

SERVES 2

Salt, for rimming glasses

2 oz simple syrup (page 141), plus more for rimming glasses

½ cup fresh cilantro leaves, plus more for garnish

5 oz reposado tequila

4 oz fresh lime juice

1 generous barspoon orange liqueur

2 fresh or dehydrated lime wheels, for garnish

I am a margarita girl! There are countless variations to this beloved cocktail, and the cilantro margarita is one of my all-time favorites. I first discovered this delicious drink in Santa Ynez at S.Y. Kitchen, which is renowned for its farm-to-table fare. I immediately fell in love with it. The combination of fresh cilantro and tequila creates a perfect balance of flavors to give you all the garden vibes!

Have ready 2 rocks glasses. To salt the glass rim, spread a little salt on a flat saucer. Dampen the rim of a glass with simple syrup, then dip the rim in the salt to coat and set the glass aside. Repeat with the second glass.

In a cocktail shaker, combine the cilantro, tequila, lime juice, simple syrup, and orange liqueur and muddle together until the cilantro is broken up and its flavors are released. Fill the shaker with ice, cover, and shake vigorously for at least 30 seconds to blend and chill the ingredients. This step is crucial, as the water from the ice needs to dilute the ingredients.

Fill the prepared glasses with ice and strain the cocktail evenly into the glasses. Garnish each glass with a lime wheel and cilantro and serve at once.

HABANERO WHISKEY SOUR

SERVES 4

FOR THE HABANERO
SIMPLE SYRUP

½ cup water

½ cup sugar

1 habanero chile

FOR THE COCKTAILS

5 oz whiskey

4 oz fresh lemon juice

2 oz fresh orange juice

2 oz habanero simple syrup

1 large egg white

4 dehydrated orange slices
or orange twists, for garnish

I love adding heat to recipes, and I have found that habanero chile and a whiskey sour are a great match. Here, I infuse simple syrup with the chile and then use the syrup to give the cocktail just a little kick of spice.

To make the simple syrup, in a small saucepan over medium heat, combine the water, sugar, and chile and bring to a simmer, stirring constantly until the sugar fully dissolves. This will take 5–10 minutes. Remove from the heat, let cool completely, and then remove and discard the chile. You will need only 2 oz of the syrup for this recipe. Store the remaining syrup in a tightly capped jar in the refrigerator for up to 4 weeks.

To make the cocktails, in a cocktail shaker, combine the whiskey, lemon juice, orange juice, simple syrup, egg white, and 1 cup ice. Cover and shake vigorously for at least 30 seconds to blend and chill the ingredients.

Drop a large ice cube into each of 4 rocks glasses. Strain the cocktail evenly into the glasses. Garnish each glass with an orange slice and serve at once.

FROZEN MOJITO

6 oz frozen limeade concentrate (½ container)

6 oz white rum

2 oz fresh lime juice

⅓ cup fresh mint leaves, plus more for garnish

4 cups crushed ice

3–4 lime wheels or wedges, for garnish

Sip on this cool cocktail and transport yourself to a tropical paradise any time of year! Refreshing, citrusy, and lusciously flavored, frozen mojitos are a perfect party drink. While always delicious for an alfresco cocktail hour, these minty drinks are equally as enjoyable to brighten a winter evening.

In a blender, combine the frozen limeade, rum, lime juice, mint, and ice and blend on high speed until smooth.

Divide evenly among 3–4 glasses and garnish each glass with mint leaves and a lime wedge. If you have cocktail umbrellas on hand, add one to each glass for extra charm. Serve at once.

CHAMPAGNE PARTY PUNCH

SERVES 6

½ cup water

½ cup firmly packed light brown sugar

4–5 lemons

1 cup rum or gin, plus more as needed

1 ½ cups raspberries

2 cups Champagne, chilled

Offering punch at a party is nice, as you can let your friends serve themselves. A punch also looks fun and festive on the table. This recipe is great with either rum or gin; give each a try and see what you prefer.

First, make a brown sugar simple syrup: In a small saucepan over medium heat, combine the water and sugar and bring to a simmer, stirring constantly until the sugar fully dissolves. This will take 5–10 minutes. Remove from the heat and let cool completely.

Using a vegetable peeler, remove the peel from 2 lemons and drop the peels into a punch bowl. Juice the 2 peeled lemons, then juice the remaining 2–3 lemons as needed to yield 1 cup juice.

Add the lemon juice, ½ cup of the cooled simple syrup, the rum, and raspberries to the punch bowl and stir gently to mix. Muddle the raspberries a little to release their flavor. Add ice cubes to the bowl, then pour in the Champagne and stir gently. Taste the punch and add more simple syrup or rum if needed. Serve at once.

CONTRATTO SPRITZ

SERVES 1

2 oz Contratto Aperitif

2 oz prosecco, chilled

2 oz soda water

Thin orange slice or dehydrated orange wedge, for garnish

As much as I love an Aperol spritz, I prefer this spritz made with Contratto Aperitif. It's less sweet and less bitter, and the color, which is more of a pale yellow than a bright orange, comes from carrots and beets. The cocktail is very refreshing and super easy and quick to make for company.

Carefully fill a wineglass with ice. Add the Contratto Aperitif, prosecco, and soda water and stir gently. Garnish with an orange slice and serve at once.

EDEN'S TIP: *This is the perfect drink for a last-minute happy hour. I like to serve it with olives, marcona almonds, or a charcuterie board.*

STRAWBERRY FROSÉ

SERVES 4

2½ cups rosé, chilled

¼ cup fresh lemon juice

15 frozen strawberries

1½ tablespoons fresh
tarragon leaves

2 tablespoons sugar

2 cups crushed ice

Nerds candy or small fresh
tarragon leaves, for garnish

I've been making this flavorful frosé for many years. Unlike most frosé recipes, which call for a stint in the freezer, this one can be whipped up and served in just minutes.

In a blender, combine the rosé, lemon juice, strawberries, tarragon, sugar, and ice and blend on high speed until smooth.

Divide evenly among 4 small glasses and garnish with the candy for fun color and crunch. Serve at once.

EDEN'S TIP: *Make this cocktail a little sweeter by adding more sugar to taste.*

GARDEN GIN *and* TONIC

Floral ice cubes (page 23)

2 oz gin

4 oz tonic water

½ oz fresh lime juice

Dash of orange bitters

Small fresh herb sprigs of choice, lime wheel, and edible fresh flowers, for garnish

I was inspired by the herbs and edible flowers in my garden to add a few easy twists—floral ice cubes, fresh herb garnish, and orange bitters—to this iconic gin cocktail. While it still respects the simplicity of the classic, the presentation is just a little fancier.

Fill a highball glass with the ice cubes. Add the gin, tonic water, lime juice, and bitters and stir gently. Garnish with herb sprigs, a lime wheel, and edible flowers and serve at once.

GARDEN GIN AND TONIC BAR

Let your guests play mixologist and make their own gin and tonics. It allows them to customize their drinks according to their taste preferences and gives you a break from refilling their glasses. Set out a nice variety of spirits, citrus juices, and garnishes along with floral ice cubes (page 23), glasses, and the necessary bar tools.

Spirits: Botanical gin, purple gin, elderflower liqueur, orange bitters

Fresh citrus juices: Grapefruit, orange, lime

Garnishes: Fresh herb sprigs (cilantro, mint, rosemary, thyme), edible fresh flowers, citrus wheels or wedges (lime, orange, lemon), berries

FLORAL SANGRIA

10 strawberries, hulled and sliced lengthwise

1 cup raspberries

1 orange, sliced

1 lemon, sliced

1 bottle (750 ml) Sauvignon Blanc

½ cup elderflower liqueur

¼ cup Cointreau

½ cup flavored sparkling water, such as raspberry, lemon, lime, or orange, plus more if needed

Mint sprigs, for garnish

This delicious and colorful sangria is a crowd pleaser. Make it the night before serving so the fruits are infused with the flavors of the wine and elderflower liqueur.

In a pitcher, combine the strawberries, raspberries, and orange and lemon slices. Pour in the Sauvignon Blanc, elderflower liqueur, and Cointreau and stir to mix. Cover and refrigerate for at least 1 hour or up to overnight.

When ready to serve, add ice to the pitcher, pour in the sparkling water, stir briefly to mix, garnish with mint sprigs, and serve.

EDEN'S TIP: *Before serving, be sure to taste the sangria and add more of any ingredient you think it needs to customize the flavor.*

MANGO MULE

SERVES 4

**FOR THE GINGER
SIMPLE SYRUP**

½ cup ginger juice

½ cup sugar

FOR THE COCKTAILS

8 oz unsweetened mango juice

8 oz vodka

8 oz ginger beer

3 oz fresh lime juice

2 oz ginger simple syrup

4 dehydrated lime wheels, for
garnish

Candied or crystallized ginger,
for garnish

Mint sprigs, for garnish

A classic Moscow mule will always be among my top five favorite cocktails. But I also like to switch it up to create a fun flavor twist. This mango version is so delicious, you can leave out the vodka and serve it as a mocktail.

To make the simple syrup, in a small saucepan over medium heat, combine the ginger juice and sugar and bring to a simmer, stirring constantly until the sugar fully dissolves. This will take 5–10 minutes. Remove from the heat and let cool completely. You will need only 2 oz of the syrup for this recipe. Store the remaining syrup in a tightly capped jar in the refrigerator for up to 5 days.

To make the cocktails, in a pitcher, combine the mango juice, vodka, ginger beer, lime juice, and simple syrup and stir to mix well.

Fill 4 copper mugs with ice. Divide the mango mixture evenly among the mugs. Garnish each with a lime wheel, candied ginger, and mint sprigs and serve at once.

LEMON–LIME SPRITZ

SERVES 2

Pink salt and lime wedge,
for salting the rim

2 oz fresh lime juice

2 oz fresh lemon juice

2 oz simple syrup (page 141)

6 oz club soda

2 dehydrated lime wheels,
for garnish

When I created this drink, I couldn't believe how much it tasted like a refreshing margarita without the tequila. This is a great mocktail that's perfect to serve any time of the year. Don't skip the salted rim. It makes this drink!

Have ready 2 rocks glasses. To salt the glass rim, spread a little pink salt on a flat saucer. Run the lime wedge around the rim of a glass, then dip the rim in the salt to coat and set the glass aside. Repeat with the second glass.

In a cocktail shaker, combine the lime juice, lemon juice, simple syrup, and club soda, cover, and shake vigorously for 20 seconds.

Fill the prepared glasses with ice and strain the drink evenly into the glasses. Garnish each drink with a lime wheel and serve at once.

BUTTERFLY PEA FLOWER LEMONADE

SERVES 6

4 cups water

¾ cup sugar

3 tablespoons dried
butterfly pea flowers

1 cup fresh lemon juice

Lemon slices, for garnish

Dried butterfly pea flowers are the magic ingredient that gives this drink its stunning shade of purple. Buy the flowers online to have on hand for making festive drinks like this for any of your gatherings. Also, those cute little butterflies are edible, another online purchase I love to have on hand.

In a saucepan over low heat, combine 1 cup of the water, the sugar, and the flowers and bring to a simmer, stirring constantly until the sugar dissolves. Continue to simmer, stirring often, until the mixture turns medium to dark blue. Remove from the heat and let cool completely.

In a pitcher, combine the remaining 3 cups water and the lemon juice. Strain the butterfly pea flower mixture through a fine-mesh sieve into the pitcher and discard the solids. Stir to mix well.

Fill the pitcher with ice, garnish with lemon slices, and serve.

> EDEN'S TIP: *This drink can be made up to 2 days before serving, minus adding the ice. Cover and store it in the refrigerator. When you're ready to serve, fill the pitcher with ice and enjoy.*
>
> *You can make this drink into a cocktail by adding 1 cup vodka with the lemon juice.*

PINK HOT CHOCOLATE

SERVES 6

4 cups whole milk

2 tablespoons honey

½ teaspoon salt

9 oz white chocolate chips

2 teaspoons beet powder or
2 tablespoons pure beet juice

1 tablespoon pure vanilla extract

¼ teaspoon freshly grated
nutmeg

Large marshmallows, for garnish

Rich and creamy, this eye-catching hot chocolate is made with white chocolate chips and beet powder. You can use pure beet juice in place of the powder to get a light pink color. The freshly grated nutmeg is a must, so make sure you add it.

In a saucepan over low heat, combine the milk, honey, and salt and bring to a simmer, whisking constantly to prevent scorching. Remove the pan from the heat and add the white chocolate chips and beet powder. Let sit for 20–30 seconds to allow the chips to soften, and then whisk until smooth and creamy.

Add the vanilla and nutmeg and whisk to mix well. Divide the hot chocolate evenly among 6 mugs, garnish with marshmallows, and serve at once.

PINEAPPLE-STRAWBERRY AGUA FRESCA

SERVES 6

2 cups pineapple chunks
(about ½ pineapple)

1 cup strawberries, hulled

½ cup sugar

2-inch piece fresh ginger,
peeled and coarsely chopped

5 cups water

Candied or crystallized ginger,
for garnish

A favorite of mine, this fruit-rich, lightly sweetened drink has a fluffy, cloud-like texture and is the most stunning shade of pink. It is great for serving anytime of the year for so many different gatherings, from baby showers to girls' dinners to kids' parties.

In a blender, combine the pineapple, strawberries, sugar, ginger, and water and blend on high speed until smooth.

Strain the frothy mixture through a fine-mesh sieve into a pitcher and discard any solids in the sieve. Fill 6 small glasses with ice and divide the agua fresca evenly among them. Garnish with candied ginger and serve at once.

> EDEN'S TIP: *Make this agua fresca the night before and store it in the refrigerator. Before serving, return the drink to the blender and blend on high speed just long enough to bring back its foam and froth.*

Four Ways to Use a Tiered Serving Tray

I've always been drawn to classic design when it comes to parties. No matter the theme, I will find a way to make it classy. Tiers have an approachable elegance, and I've used tiered trays hundreds of times over the past decade.

Most popularly associated with afternoon tea, three-tier trays are a staple of entertaining because they make it easy to serve food in a small space, add height to the table, and double as a great centerpiece. I've had the same galvanized one for a long time, use it year-round, and have gotten creative with it. You can make a whole party on a three-tier tray! If you don't have one, you should get one. It will last your lifetime and will never go out of style.

SEAFOOD TIERS

WHAT TO ADD

Seafood: Crab legs, raw oysters on the half shell, jumbo shrimp, and lobster claws, arranged on a bed of ice

Sauces: Melted butter, cocktail sauce, prepared horseradish, Sriracha mayonnaise, and Green Mignonette Sauce (recipe follows)

Extras: Grilled or steamed corn on the cob, Old Bay seasoning, and lemon wedges

I grew up in a small coastal town, my grandfather was a local commercial fisherman, and our family spent a lot of time at my grandparents' house. After being out on the water all day, my grandfather would come home in the early evening with a bucketful of live crabs—always an exciting surprise for us. My grandmother would immediately start to prepare them, and I would just as quickly run out of the room in horror. But then we would all have dinner together, with newspapers spread on the table and plenty of melted butter to accompany the delicious boiled crabs.

I've taken those early family memories of crab feasts a step further and nowadays, I create a beautiful seafood tier. It's an enjoyable way to entertain guests for a small gathering, especially if there is an abundance of sauces and dips. Here is what I like to serve, but think of this list as inspiration and add or omit items to make it your own seafood tier. The exception is the melted butter—it's essential!

GREEN MIGNONETTE SAUCE

MAKES ABOUT 1¼ CUPS

1 cup rice vinegar

Juice of ½ lemon

2 tablespoons finely chopped shallot

1 tablespoon seeded and finely chopped jalapeño chile

¼ cup finely chopped fresh flat-leaf parsley

In a small bowl, combine the vinegar, lemon juice, shallot, chile, and parsley and mix well. (Or combine all the ingredients in a jar, cap tightly, and shake to mix.) Cover and chill for at least 30 minutes before using. The sauce will keep in the fridge for up to 1 month.

EDEN'S TIP: *Shop for fresh seafood at your local seafood market or farmers' market for the best options, and keep everything cold until just before serving. Set out bowls for discarded shells, cocktail picks for pulling meat from legs and claws, and plenty of napkins and wet wipes.*

HOT DOG TIERS

WHAT TO ADD

Grilled hot dogs

Hot dogs buns

Fixings: Ketchup, mustard, mayonnaise, pickle relish, chopped onions, chopped jalapeño chiles, and sauerkraut

If you're hosting a barbecue or bonfire, this is a fun way to serve hot dogs and all the fixings. Set out some drinks and bags of potato chips and your meal is complete.

MINI BAR TIERS

WHAT TO ADD

Spirits and wines: Miniature bottles of spirits and premade cocktails, and splits or half bottles of wine

Extras: Ice; bottles of tonic water, soda water, or other mixers; half bottles of water; and citrus peel strips, fruit slices, olives, cocktail onions, herbs, or other garnishes, all placed nearby for guests to add to their drinks

There is no particular story about how this idea came to me aside from that I love mini anything, and it seems my guests do too. Mini is simply charming, right? Plus, an entire tiered serving tray filled with mini drinks would be perfect for a party, and so here we are.

I love this idea for a gathering: let guests pick what they want and have fun mixing up their beverage.

ICE CREAM TIERS

WHAT TO ADD

Ice cream: Offer a few different flavors so guests have a choice. I like to add low-sugar and vegan options as well.

Toppings: Set out a nice variety, such as whipped cream, hot fudge sauce, caramel sauce, nuts, different kinds of sprinkles, and cherries.

If I don't have time to make a dessert for a gathering, I prepare an ice cream board with toppings and present it to my guests to assemble their own servings. The idea of an ice cream tiered tray arose when I hosted a small party and planned to serve ice cream outside. However, I wanted to give all of us more time, so I grabbed my three-tier tray, put ice on the bottom tier, set the ice cream atop the ice, and then filled the upper tiers with all the toppings. It was the perfect solution, and the presentation looked great. Ice cream tier forever!

MORE IDEAS FOR TIERED TRAYS

S'mores Tiers, Dessert Tiers, Hot Cocoa Tiers, Cheese and Charcuterie Tiers, Sushi Tiers, Take-out Food Tiers, Sandwich Tiers, Brunch Tiers, Tea Party Tiers

Making
Gatherings
Special

I'm all about keeping it simple on most occasions. Still, I love hosting memorable gatherings for friends and family, and I love a theme. Whether it's a birthday party, a baby shower, a holiday get-together, or the beginning of a new season, I'm always looking for ways to make it unique. The best parties have thoughtful details that give each guest an unforgettable experience. These small touches, from a signature cocktail in a beautiful glass to delectable food served on attractive plates, will make your party feel luxurious and special.

Creating an inviting atmosphere with music, cozy seating arrangements, and natural pathways from drinks to food to quiet conversation spots is crucial to setting the right ambiance. Keep the decor simple but welcoming—perhaps a couple of lovely flower arrangements and some strategically placed votives.

Gatherings are essential to fostering deeper connections with your friends and family. When we make the time to get together, it's not just about the food or decorations. It's about taking the time to reconnect, catch up, and enjoy one another's company. Hosting a gathering can be as simple as having drinks and snacks with close friends or going all out with an extravagant dinner party. Either way, it's essential to devote the time necessary to create those special moments that bring us closer together.

IT'S ALL ABOUT HYGGE

Hosting a hygge party is not just about throwing a cozy get-together. It is about creating an atmosphere of warmth and contentment. Hygge is a Danish concept that focuses on enjoying the simple pleasures in life with loved ones. To host a hygge party, every element should contribute to a sense of comfort and relaxation. Here are a few tips I've used over the years to create a cozy space for entertaining.

CANDLES

Candles have been used for centuries for both light and to produce a warm, inviting atmosphere. The ancient Romans set them out for religious ceremonies and celebrations, and before the invention of electric lighting, they were used to light homes during long winter nights in Europe, the Middle East, and beyond.

Today, the gentle flicker of candlelight creates a calming and welcoming ambiance for entertaining. The soft light provides the ideal warm and convivial atmosphere for a dinner party or other special occasion and perfectly sets the mood when romance is on the calendar.

You can choose from different types of candles. Unscented votives are great lined up and down the center of a dinner table, while scented candles are perfect for spaces like living rooms and even restrooms. I love to use tall, slender taper candles and beautiful holders to add height to a table.

Invest in a few beautiful candleholders and buy inexpensive votives online. I add charm to votives by decoupaging dried flowers to the outside (see page 198).

CANDLE CARE KIT

I've had experiences where a candle burns smoky, it won't fit into the holder, or it leans to one side. Here are the tools and tricks you need to make using candles problem-free.

Wick trimmer: Trimming the wick of a candle with this simple, sharp tool helps control the flame size and prevents excess smoke from forming.

Snuffer: This long-handled tool with a hollow cone on the end is a great way to extinguish candles without any wax-splattering risk.

Candle sharpener: Used much like a hand pencil sharpener, a candle sharpener will shave the base of a taper candle so it will fit snugly into a candleholder. A candle properly seated in a holder also helps keep the wick centered while the candle burns. Additionally, a sharpener can be used to trim away excess wax buildup that accumulates at the base of the candle, giving your candle a cleaner look and a more efficient burn.

Candle adhesive: This specially formulated adhesive is used to keep candles standing straight up in their holders. It is especially handy if the candle is a bit too small for the holder, as it will keep it securely upright.

Electric candle lighter: These lighters are gold! They're inexpensive and rechargeable, and I keep one in several areas of my home so I don't have to chase down matches.

FLORAL VOTIVE DIY

You'll need dried flowers, votives, Mod Podge, and a Mod Podge paintbrush. To decorate each votive, follow these simple steps.

- Brush a light layer of Mod Podge on the entire outside of a votive and stick a few dried flowers onto the votive.

- Brush a second light layer of Mod Podge over the flowers and around the entire outside of the votive. Mod Podge leaves a texture, so make sure you swipe the entire outside of the candle to make the surface consistent. Let the votive dry overnight before using.

FLOWERS

You can't have a party without flowers. I know some people say to keep it simple and skip the flowers, but I'm here to tell you this is unacceptable! Flowers are *key* to creating a charming atmosphere. Here are some tips for creating floral arrangements for parties:

- Use bud vases. This way, you add just a few flowers to each vase, and no arranging is required.

- Use just one type of flower in a vase. This is one of the best tricks! You don't need a variety to make a stunning arrangement. For example, use all white roses in a cylinder glass vase, or slip some lilac branches into a tall, slim vase.

- Get creative with the vessels. Here are some I've used: teacups, bowls, mason jars, empty coffee cans and tea tins, ice buckets, galvanized buckets, pitchers, and old candle jars. Whatever you use, be sure to clean it well with soap and water to remove any bacteria before you repurpose it for flowers.

- To ready the flowers, whether picked from your garden or purchased, remove any leaves that will fall below the water line once the flowers are in their container. Then give each flower stem a diagonal cut. If the flowers have a woody stem, use a knife to make an angled cut at the bottom, then slice upward as you continue cutting. This allows for more water absorption.

- Fill the container about three-fourths full with fresh, cool water, then add the flowers. To keep the flowers fresh, add water daily as needed to refill to the original level. After two or three days, change the water and cut the stems again before returning the flowers to the container.

- Keep the flowers in a cool area and out of direct sunlight to prevent wilting. If you're hosting outside during the day, wait until the last minute to carry the flowers outdoors.

LIGHTING

Lighting is everything! When we designed our house, we made sure every light switch was on a dimmer. This way, you can lower the lights for a moodier vibe. I can't remember any gathering I've ever hosted where the lights were fully turned on.

Use warm lighting, nothing too harsh or blue. You can easily trade out your light bulbs and add dimmers to your switches. Taking the time to create pleasant lighting makes such a difference not only when entertaining but also every day.

Outside, I use market lights, also known as string lights, on dimmers. They add so much charm and coziness to the space, and they can be used year-round.

MUSIC

You can create any mood you want for your gathering with music. It plays a crucial role in providing the perfect vibe and setting a welcoming atmosphere. Music evokes emotions, brings people together, and yields memorable experiences. I prefer to keep my music simple and easy to access, so I use a playlist on a music streaming service. An array of good streaming services, such as Spotify, Apple, and Amazon, are available today, which makes it easy to find a playlist for any music genre or theme you are seeking for your event.

THROW A FAUX SHEEPSKIN ON IT!

The versatile faux sheepskin—I love it just as much as I love flowers. OK, maybe not as much as flowers. But you will find a couple of sheepskins—or maybe more—at most of my gatherings all year round. They contribute warmth and texture to any setting, and I like to use them in a variety of roles.

They are incredibly soft and comfortable and perfect for cloaking seating areas, whether they be chairs, haystacks, metal outdoor furniture, or even swings. Sheepskins can be rugs or artfully arranged decorations, or they can cover anything you don't want guests to see, such as a wine stain on your garden furniture. Plus, faux sheepskins, unlike genuine sheepskins, are affordable. They are also very durable, so you can use them often and they won't wear out quickly. They are easy to clean too. I toss them into the washing machine and let them air-dry outside.

HYDRATION STATION

The gift of hydration! I want my guests to leave feeling good, especially the next day, so I always have a small area where they can grab water during the gathering. I like small glass water bottles (over plastic) or pitchers of water with sliced fruit. Here are some other ways I add charm to my hydration station:

- Flat and sparkling water
- Hydration packets (electrolyte powder) for guests to add to their water bottles for extra hydration
- Lemon wedges
- Paper or bamboo straws

CONVERSATION STARTERS AND GAMES

Conversation starters are one of my party tricks. If it is time to divert a conversation or to keep things rolling, I'll pull out my conversation cards. Each card has a thought-provoking question, funny or serious, for guests to answer. It's a great way to get to know people better too.

Games are also a great way to bring people together. Tailor your choice of games—from board games, card games, and yard games to charades and trivia and more—to the crowd playing them and the party. Guessing games like Heads Up and Pictionary are always fun and are a good way to break the ice.

Themed Parties

Most of the time when I'm entertaining, it's pretty simple. I invite a few couples over, and we snack on apps and sip homemade cocktails. However, I like a theme for special occasions, so I highlighted a few party ideas you can re-create throughout the year. A bonfire is perfect year-round. In the winter, have extra-cozy blankets and warm drinks available. The harvest moon party can be altered to mark a change in the seasons or a new beginning. I especially love this idea around New Year's too. Movie nights can also be brought indoors in the winter, but always use a projector to make it unique. The garden party is great for spring, summer, or fall. It's a beautiful theme for celebrations such as baby and bridal showers, Mother's Day, and birthday parties.

CHERISH YOUR VISION; CHERISH YOUR IDEALS;
CHERISH THE MUSIC THAT STIRS IN YOUR HEART.
THE BEAUTY THAT FORMS IN YOUR MIND.
THE LO⟨VELINESS THAT DR⟩APES YOUR PUREST THOUGHTS.
⟨...⟩ YOUR WORLD WILL AT LAST BE BUILT.

GARDEN PARTY

When I was a child, our family briefly lived in a small house that looked out at the ocean and had a vast open field in the back. Inside, the house was a little chaotic, so to escape, I would ride my bike deep into nature, where I would surround myself with wildflowers and ladybugs for hours. This is where I always felt at home and at peace.

Growing up, I never got to attend or host garden parties, but that hasn't stopped me as an adult! After more than thirteen years of being the CEO of *Sugar and Charm*, I've attended and hosted my fair share of garden gatherings. They are as good as I envisioned them.

A garden party can be held anytime from spring until the end of fall in Southern California. When plants are blooming, it is always nice to take your get-together outside. Plus, a garden gathering is the perfect way to celebrate any occasion, from a birthday to an anniversary to a graduation to just because. It's fun to enjoy quality time with friends in your outdoor oasis—big or small— while savoring delicious food and drinks.

GARDEN PARTY PLANNING

SET THE MOOD

- **Terra-cotta pots** filled with herbs and flowers for the centerpiece
- **Votives** with decoupage dried flowers
- **Table settings** of beautiful dinnerware, flatware, and glassware
- One or two **seed packets** at each table setting
- **Paper lanterns** for extra decor and lighting

SIGNATURE DRINKS

- Butterfly Pea Flower Lemonade (page 176)
- Garden Gin and Tonic (page 168)
- Lemon Drop (page 155)

FOOD

- Whipped Ricotta Crostini Served Three Ways (page 30)
- Roasted Carrot Hummus with Chile Crunch (page 46)
- Orange Buttermilk Dip with Seasonal Vegetables (page 38)
- Creamy Pea Pasta with Crispy Prosciutto (page 92)
- Almond Snacking Cake with Berries (page 135)
- Super-Simple Buttermilk Ice (page 128)

ACTIVITIES

- Make-your-own Garden Gin and Tonic Bar (page 168)
- Create your flower arrangement. Or, set up a make-your-own flower arrangement area with cut flowers and greens, vases and other containers, and necessary tools for guests to create their own flower arrangements
- Yard games, such as bocce or cornhole, to get everyone involved
- Conversation starters
- Garden class on incorporating native and pollinator plants in home gardens

EXTRAS

- Essential oils and natural bug repellents
- Market lights
- Seed packets and terra-cotta planters for party favors

GARDEN GIN AND TONIC BAR

Let your guests play mixologist and make their own gin and tonics. This allows them to customize their drink according to their taste preferences and gives you a break from refilling their glasses. Set out a well-stocked bar that includes a variety of spirits, citrus juices, and garnishes, plus plenty of floral ice cubes (page 23), glasses, and bar tools.

BAR TOOLS

Jigger, barspoon, glass bottles (for syrups and juices), highball glasses, full ice bucket

SPIRITS

Botanical gin, purple gin, elderflower liqueur, orange bitters

FRESH CITRUS JUICES

Grapefruit, orange, blood orange, lime, yuzu

TONIC WATER

Plain and flavored (such as elderflower or citrus)

GARNISHES

Fresh herb sprigs (mint, rosemary, thyme), edible fresh flowers, citrus wheels or wedges (lime, orange, lemon), berries (raspberries, blackberries)

EXTRAS

Flavored syrups, shrubs (fruit-infused vinegars), assorted bitters to encourage guests to experiment

BONFIRE PARTY

When it comes to bonfires, I have a lot of special memories. I spent many summers in Ohio, where we would catch and release lightning bugs and stay up late with a big fire. When the smoke would start to come our way, we would say "fuzzy bunnies," which supposedly made the smoke shift direction— and sometimes it did. I tried this as an adult, but it has never had the same effect. We would also make campfire pies, heating a mixture of berries, lemon juice, and sugar sandwiched between bread slices in long-handled sandwich irons on the fire, and to this day, it's one of my favorite desserts. I always loved the coziness of being outside too.

An excellent choice for summer and fall, a bonfire party is a fun way to entertain guests without having to make an entire dinner. Instead, invite friends for an evening of warmth, drinks, snacks, and dessert. To make it memorable, dress up the party area with charming decorations and organize some fun activities. When you're planning a bonfire party, be sure not to build fires on windy days and check for any local regulations.

BONFIRE PARTY PLANNING

SET THE MOOD

· **Baskets** of cozy blankets and faux sheepskin throws

· **Light the scene** with outdoor candle lanterns and dimmable electric lanterns

· Flower arrangements in **rustic containers**

· Stacks of **wood**

· **Camping-inspired** mugs, utensils, and napkins

SIGNATURE DRINKS

· Pink Hot Chocolate (page 179)

· Mango Mule (page 172)

· Cooler filled with sparkling water

FOOD

· Cheese platter (page 26)

· Classied-Up S'mores

· High-quality chocolate, large marshmallows, berries, Nutella or caramel and other spreads, graham crackers or Pizzelle wafer cookies

· Buttered popcorn

· Chocolate Cherry Chunk Cookies (page 120)

ACTIVITIES

· Storytelling

· Games such as Pictionary or charades

· Stargazing

EXTRAS

· S'more kits—Make homemade gift bags or baskets with graham crackers, marshmallows, and chocolate bars

· Bug repellent

· Neon bracelets

· Flashlights or other all-purpose lighters

How to Elevate Your S'mores

· Purchase gourmet marshmallows: think large, fluffy marshmallows in a variety of flavors

· Try artisanal chocolate bars with distinctive ingredients such as lavender, citrus, or dark chocolate

· Add Pizzelle cookies as a graham cracker alternative

· Provide optional spreads like Nutella, lemon curd, or pumpkin butter

· Cut up candy bars, like Snickers, MilkyWay, or Twix, for a unique twist on the traditional Hershey's bar

· Add a touch of freshness by including ripe berries

HARVEST MOON PARTY

The past few years, I've studied a lot about mindfulness and have taken up meditation and journaling. It's been such an awakening for me, and that journey has inspired this party. I also like the start of a new season and I love New Year's, a time to set goals and my intentions.

So I created my version of a harvest moon party, which celebrates the autumnal equinox, when the sun and the moon align perfectly. This happens at the end of September, and it offers an excellent opportunity to have friends over to reset, journal, set intentions, and support one another.

Look on it as a time to journal and to meditate on the changing of the season. Encourage your guests to take a few moments to write down their thoughts or reflections in a special notebook. If they need some guidance, give them ideas and ask questions about their goals and intentions, or if they quickly grasp the idea, offer them support in their new adventures. This gathering has a lot of meaning and purpose, so it's essential to focus on the deeper aspects of the evening.

HARVEST MOON PARTY PLANNING

SET THE MOOD

· Cozy **faux sheepskins**
· **Tiered candle holders**
· **Dried sage bundles** and **palo santo sticks** (make sure the latter are responsibly sourced)
· **Bud vase florals**

SIGNATURE COCKTAIL

· Habanero Whiskey Sour (page 159)

FOOD

· Charcuterie Served Three Ways (page 42)
· Ricotta-Stuffed Pasta Shells (page 79)
· Lois's Bacon Salad with Warm Bacon Vinaigrette (page 66)
· Brown Sugar–Rosemary Shortbread Cookies (page 127)

ACTIVITIES

· Journaling
· Making vision boards
· Making affirmation cards
· Sitting meditation
· Sharing a sound bath

EXTRAS

· Take-home journals
· Dried sage bundles or palo santo sticks
· Permanent jewelry
· Work with a professional to weld a bracelet for your guests to signify a special event or bond in your life.

FONDUE PARTY

I'm a big fan of fondue because, hello, melted cheese! But it also allows for creativity, fun, and interaction. It's ideal for any occasion, whether a family get-together, a cocktail party, a low-key gathering with friends, or a romantic date night.

I like to dip small cubes of crusty French bread into the fondue, but some people prefer apple or pear slices or raw or lightly steamed vegetables, such as broccoli or cauliflower florets, celery sticks, or asparagus.

Fondue is not just for winter either. This is a year-round party idea you can host outside. Set the mood with cozy candles, faux sheepskins for added warmth, and a centerpiece of fresh flowers.

EDEN'S TIP: *Each guest is outfitted with a fondue fork that is used only for dipping, not for eating. Once the bread cube or other dipper has been dipped and swirled in the cheese, it is slipped off the fork onto a small plate and eaten with a regular fork.*

FONDUE PARTY PLANNING

SET THE MOOD

· Candle **lanterns**
· **Faux sheepskins** and pillows
· Arrangements of **fresh flowers**
· Wool **blankets**

SIGNATURE COCKTAILS

· White wine or Champagne
· Lemon Drop (page 155)
· Contratto Spritz (page 164)

FOOD

· Cheese fondue (see recipe)
· Colorful vegetable platter
· Lois's Bacon Salad with Warm Bacon Vinaigrette (page 66)
· Chocolate Espresso Cupcakes with Espresso Buttercream (page 123)
· Swiss chocolate bars

ACTIVITIES

· Table topics
· Trivia game
· Chocolate tasting
· Card games

CHEESE FONDUE

SERVES 4

13 oz Gruyère cheese, coarsely shredded or cut into small cubes

6 oz Emmentaler cheese, coarsely shredded or cut into small cubes

1½ tablespoons cornstarch

¾ cup dry white wine

1 teaspoon fresh lemon juice

1 clove garlic, grated (use a citrus grater)

⅛ teaspoon ground nutmeg

Crusty French bread (cut into cubes), small boiled potatoes, steamed vegetables, cured meats, and fruits of choice, for dipping

In a bowl, combine the Gruyère and Emmentaler cheeses and toss with the cornstarch, coating the cheeses evenly. (Coating the cheeses with cornstarch helps them to melt smoothly.)

In a fondue pot or heavy saucepan, combine the wine, lemon juice, garlic, and nutmeg and bring just to a simmer over medium heat. Gradually add the cheese mixture and cook, stirring constantly, just until all the cheese has melted.

Serve with cubed bread, crusty bread, small boiled potatoes, steamed vegetables like broccoli and cauliflower, cured meats, or fruits like apples and pears.

OUTDOOR MOVIE NIGHT

The first time we set up an outdoor movie night in the backyard with our kids was magical. The juxtaposition of a movie playing on an outdoor screen and the stars above gave me loads of good feelings. I might have looked at the stars more than the film, but I know for sure the night was special.

This party is inspired by that magical evening spent outside. Invite friends and kids over for a family movie night. Include plenty of pillows and blankets and invest in a good projector!

OUTDOOR MOVIE NIGHT PLANNING

SET THE MOOD

· Candle **lanterns**

· Faux sheepskins, **throw pillows,** bean bags, and floor cushions

· Fresh **flowers**

· Movie **projector**

SIGNATURE DRINKS

· Fizzy Cucumber Gimlet (page 149)

· Pink Hot Chocolate (page 179)

FOOD

· Cheese platter (page 26)

· Chocolate Popcorn Bark (page 131)

· Vintage candy board (page 98)

· Bowls of popcorn

ACTIVITIES

· Screening of a favorite seasonal movie

· Movie trivia

· Jenga Giant

· Popcorn Bar (page 53)

PARTY MENU GUIDE

TEA PARTY: Fizzy Cucumber Gimlet (page 149), Mussels in Buttery Miso Broth (page 34), Sesame Pasta Slaw (page 65), Peanut Butter Noodles with Shredded Chicken (page 87), Almond Snacking Cake with Berries (page 135), and Brown Sugar–Rosemary Shortbread Cookies (page 127).

BABY SHOWER: Contratto Spritz (page 164), Butterfly Pea Flower Lemonade (page 176), Yogurt Tahini Dip (page 50), Roasted Carrot Hummus with Chile Crunch (page 46), Charcuterie Served Three Ways (page 42), Broccoli Quiche with Homemade Buttery Crust (page 88), and Banana Pudding Trifles with Fluffy Marshmallow Topping (page 108).

BIRTHDAY PARTY: Champagne Party Punch (page 163), cheese platter (page 26), Whipped Ricotta Crostini Served Three Ways (page 30), Ricotta-Stuffed Pasta Shells (page 79), Lois's Bacon Salad with Warm Bacon Vinaigrette (page 66), Sprinkle Cake with Swiss Meringue Buttercream (page 112), and vintage candy board (page 98).

CINCO DE MAYO: Cilantro Margarita (page 156), Pineapple-Strawberry Agua Fresca (page 180), Cilantro-Lime Corn Salad with Cotija Cheese (page 69), Queso Fundido with Kielbasa (page 37), Slow Cooker Pork Tacos and Taco Bar (page 83), and Shortbread Crumble Bars with Fruit Preserves (page 100).

FALL GATHERING: Habanero Whiskey Sour (page 159), Roasted Carrot Hummus with Chile Crunch (page 46), Marinated Goat Cheese (page 49), Orange-Cranberry Corn Bread with Cardamom (page 62), and Chocolate Cherry Chunk Cookies (page 120).

SPRING GATHERING: Floral Sangria (page 171), Garden Gin and Tonic (page 168), Marinated Goat Cheese (page 49), Whipped Ricotta Crostini Served Three Ways (page 30), Year-Round Herby Lemon Pasta (page 84), Broccoli Quiche with Homemade Buttery Crust (page 88), Almond Snacking Cake with Berries (page 135), and Super-Simple Buttermilk Ice (page 128).

GAME DAY: Ham and Cheese Sliders (page 29), Fancy Homemade Onion Dip (page 41) with vegetable dippers, Lois's Bacon Salad with Warm Bacon Vinaigrette (page 66), Southern Cheese and Charcuterie Board (page 95), Peanut Butter Rice Krispie Treats (page 116), and Coconut Oil Chocolate Chip Cookies (page 107).

POOL PARTY: Frozen Mojito (page 160), Prosecco Slushy Pops with Strawberry and Peach (page 152), Melon Bar with Whipped Feta (page 73), Orange Buttermilk Dip with Seasonal Vegetables (page 38), Ham and Cheese Sliders (page 29), Chopped Salad with Citrus-Cumin Dressing (page 70), and ice cream cookie sandwiches (page 98).

RANDOM FRIDAY NIGHT: Mango Mule (page 172), Popcorn Bar (page 53), simple arugula salad, Vodka Baked Rigatoni with Italian Sausage Meatballs (page 91), and ice cream soda floats (page 98).

SUNDAY BRUNCH: Lemon Drop (page 155), Peaches, Blue Cheese, and Prosciutto charcuterie board (page 42), Broccoli Quiche with Homemade Buttery Crust (page 88), Creamy Pea Pasta with Crispy Prosciutto (page 92), and Coconut Bundt Cake (page 103).

MEASUREMENT GUIDE

MEASUREMENTS FOR MERRY MAKING

KNOW YOUR NUMBER OF GUESTS

(6)   (12)   (24)

WINE   RED, WHITE, SPARKLING, ROSÉ

6 guests: 5–6 bottles   **12 guests:** 9–12 bottles   **24 guests:** 22–24 bottles

To be safe, I like to have 1 bottle per guest on hand.

BEER

6 guests: 4–6 six packs

12 guests: 5–7 six packs

24 guests: 10 six packs

WATER

6 guests: 3 six packs

12 guests: 4 six packs

24 guests: 5 six packs

LIQUOR
TEQUILA, RUM, VODKA, WHISKEY, GIN

6 guests: 1 bottle of each (tequila, rum, vodka) *or* 3 bottles of one for a signature cocktail

12 guests: 2 bottles of each (tequila, rum, vodka) *or* 5 bottles of one for a signature cocktail

24 guests: 3 bottles of each (tequila, rum, vodka) *or* 8 bottles of one for a signature cocktail

Each cocktail should contain about 2 oz of liquor. A 750-ml bottle holds about 25 oz, which is enough for 12 cocktails, an average of 4 to 5 drinks per person, depending on the length of the party.

MIXERS
CLUB SODA, TONIC WATER, GINGER ALE,
FRESH JUICE (DEPENDING ON COCKTAIL)

6 guests: 1 liter of each

12 guests: 2 liters of each

24 guests: 3 liters of each

NONALCOHOLIC DRINKS
SODA, JUICE, LEMONADE

6 guests: 3 gallons

12 guests: 5 gallons

24 guests: 9 gallons

or four 12-oz drinks per person

ICE ICE ICE   **6 guests:** 8 lb ice   **12 guests:** 14 lb ice   **24 guests:** 26 lb ice

GARNISHES
LEMONS, ORANGES, LIMES,
OR YOUR CHOICE

6 guests: 18–24 pieces

12 guests: 36–48 pieces

24 guests: 72–96 pieces

CHEESE AND CHARCUTERIE

6 guests: 2–3 lb cheese & 1 lb charcuterie

12 guests: 4–6 lb cheese & 2 lb charcuterie

24 guests: 10–12 lb cheese & 3 lb charcuterie

APPETIZERS

6 guests: 24–36 pieces   **12 guests:** 48–72 pieces   **24 guests:** 96–144 pieces

Plan on 4–6 pieces per guest. If you are hosting an appetizer party (rather than dinner), plan on 8 pieces per guest. It is nice to have 2 or 3 options for smaller parties and 3 to 6 options for larger gatherings.

BITE-SIZE DESSERTS

6 guests: 18–24 pieces

12 guests: 36–48 pieces

24 guests: 72–96 pieces

SNACKS   CHIPS, NUTS, CANDY

6 guests: one 16-oz bag of each

12 guests: two 16-oz bags of each

24 guests: three 16-oz bags of each

EDEN'S HANDBOOK

These are the retailers, both brick and mortar and online, where I buy most of my party supplies.

ANTHROPOLOGIE
Shop here for beautiful, colorful glassware, decorative baking items, and candles.

BURKE DECOR
I often shop for fun items for entertaining at this well-stocked online boutique.

CRATE AND BARREL
Here is another favorite of mine for hosting supplies and home goods.

EAST FORK POTTERY
Based in Asheville, North Carolina, East Fork makes pottery that is both beautiful and functional. I use their cake plates, ice cream bowls, and mugs daily. The company also makes and sells handsome platters, serving bowls, and a curated selection of hosting items.

ETSY
Great for vintage items, customizing party supplies, and sugar-coated cake toppers. I found the edible butterflies I used for the Butterfly Pea Flower Lemonade (page 176) on Etsy.

FOOD52
One of my favorite sources for unique and fun items for cooking and hosting, the online culinary platform Food52 carefully curates its selection of items, with an eye toward featuring artisanal makers.

H&M HOME
This large home decor retailer is another excellent source for stylish and inexpensive hosting items.

IKEA
If you are looking to buy well-priced yet attractive vases, glassware, serving platters, and more, Ikea offers a top-notch selection.

KANA
I love Kana's precut parchment paper, which not only saves time but is also 100 percent compostable and biodegradable. I always keep a variety of shapes and sizes on hand.

REPURPOSE
If you're hosting a large gathering and want to use disposable party goods, upgrade to biodegradable plant-based or bamboo items. The online source Repurpose has a wide selection of wonderfully designed, sustainable products.

WILLIAMS SONOMA

Williams Sonoma always has me covered whenever I need something for a dinner party or to upgrade my cooking game. They sell everything from mixers, coffee makers, and All-Clad pots to baking supplies, classic plates and serving ware, linen napkins, and sauces galore.

WORLD MARKET

A specialty import store for all things food, drink, and home, World Market is a one-stop shop for party supplies, especially around the holidays.

VINTAGE AND SECOND-HAND SHOPS

I can't tell you how many great items—from beautiful punch bowls to real China wooden boxes to all-around fabulous finds—I've discovered scouring vintage stores. The time and effort are definitely worth it. Start by checking out well-trodden local spots. I've purchased the most wonderful crystal glasses at Goodwill for a dollar each.

ACKNOWLEDGMENTS

Zan – I am eternally grateful for your unwavering support since day one. Your constant encouragement and incredible photography skills have been invaluable. Your boundless creativity never fails to inspire me, and I appreciate how you push me to be better. Thank you for always cheering me on and for taking all the gorgeous photographs in this book.

Charlene – Your endless help with *Sugar and Charm* has made my life more joyful. Your sharing of amazing recipes, grocery-shopping assistance, recipe-testing skills, and willingness to wash countless dishes have enriched my life in many ways. Your passion for cooking is undeniably inspiring, and I have learned so much from you. You truly embody the spirit of an Italian grandmother in the kitchen!

Megan – Thank you for all your work designing this book. Your attention to detail and eye for design have been of immeasurable help in bringing this project to life. I am so grateful for your patience, perseverance, and dedication throughout the process.

Elizabeth – Thank you for being a crucial part of my journey toward achieving one of my biggest dreams. Your help and support along the way have meant everything to me.

Madelyn, Kendall, and the Williams Sonoma Team – The support you two have shown me over the years has been incredible. Supplying me with every kitchen tool and prop was instrumental in making this cookbook successful. Your generosity and support have been truly invaluable.

Amy – It's been a pleasure creating this book with you and the Weldon Owen team. Thank you for your guidance and support throughout the project. Working with such a talented and dedicated team has been a dream come true.

Morgan and Alyssa – We had a fun few days of prepping, cooking, and styling. Thank you both for a beautiful and successful photo shoot. Your hard work and remarkable eye for detail have helped make this cookbook a reality.

Romeo and Monroe – I am your mom first and foremost, but you have also been my taste testers and sous chefs. Thank you for eagerly trying out all my recipes and always being willing to give me your honest opinion, even when I disagree! You both bring so much joy and laughter into my life, and I am grateful for every moment that we spend together.

All my longtime *Sugar and Charm* readers, friends, and family – You have encouraged and supported me throughout this journey, and I thank you from the bottom of my heart. Your love and your belief in me have given me the courage to pursue my passion and create this cookbook. I hope these recipes bring as much joy to your lives as they have to mine.

And finally, **a special thank-you to everyone who will read and then try the recipes in this book**. I hope these dishes will not only fill your belly but also warm your heart and create lasting memories for you and your loved ones. Happy cooking, baking, and party planning!

INDEX

weldon**owen**

an imprint of Insight Editions
P.O. Box 3088
San Rafael, CA 94912
www.weldonowen.com

CEO Raoul Goff
VP Publisher Roger Shaw
Publishing Director Katie Killebrew
Associate Publisher Amy Marr
VP Creative Chrissy Kwasnik
Art Director Megan Sinead Bingham
VP Manufacturing Alix Nicholaeff
Production Manager Joshua Smith
Sr Production Manager, Subsidiary Rights Lina s Palma-Temena

Text © 2024 Eden Passante
Photography by Zan Passante

ISBN: 979-8-88674-148-3

Manufactured in China by Insight Editions
10 9 8 7 6 5 4 3 2 1

ROOTS of PEACE   REPLANTED PAPER

Insight Editions, in association with Roots of Peace, will plant two
trees for each tree used in the manufacturing of this book. Roots of
Peace is an internationally renowned humanitarian organization
dedicated to eradicating land mines worldwide and converting
war-torn lands into productive farms and wildlife habitats. Roots
of Peace will plant two million fruit and nut trees in Afghanistan
and provide farmers there with the skills and support necessary for
sustainable land use.